SPEAK UP FOR YOURSELF

Effective oral communication for business

Christopher Beddows, MSc (Ed)

Senior Lecturer in English and Communication Studies
at Nelson and Colne College

CW00530255

PITMAN PUBLISHING
128 Long Acre, London WC2E 9AN

© Christopher Beddows 1989

First published in Great Britain 1989

British Library Cataloguing in Publication Data

Beddows, Christopher
Speak up for yourself: effective oral
communication for business.
I. Title
001.54'2

ISBN 0-273-03025-6

Typeset by Avocet, Bicester, Oxon
Printed and bound in Great Britain

Contents

Preface

There is something that is almost inherently contradictory about a book on spoken English. A book is for reading and speech is for speaking. The two are distinct and separate – or so we tend to believe. Of course, on consideration, we realise that the process of speech is vastly complicated and, although indulged in with abandon by most of us, is the product of thought, judgement, consideration and decision.

This book is intended to guide those who are studying for a career in some form of business to think, judge, consider and decide before plunging into speech. The philosophy behind the text (such as it is) is based on the premise that regardless of academic ability a student is capable of drawing on a fund of commonsense and experience in order to communicate more effectively.

For many of the exercises it will be helpful to have the use of a tape recorder, and to have access to two telephone handsets, particularly for Section 6.

Christopher Beddows

Acknowledgements

I should like to express my gratitude to Christabel Burniston of the English Speaking Board (International) Limited for all her help and advice. I should also like to thank Guardian Newspapers Limited for permission to reproduce the article by Gareth Parry in Section 4 of this book. Finally, I should like to give special thanks to my wife for her help and patience.

The need for efficient oral skills

It has been said that money is the oil that keeps the wheels of business turning. It is in fact efficient and courteous communication between individuals that keeps an organisation on a smooth and level course.

Much of the instruction given, as well as the exercises in role play and personal preparation that punctuate this text, are based simply on commonsense. Do not be insulted. If you are blessed with commonsense you will realise how important this is and how it can help you to achieve significant progress.

Although there has been an explosion in technological communications, the basic need for human beings to talk to and with each other clearly, politely, carefully and diplomatically still remains. Yet, strangely, this is accomplished with decreasing efficiency.

If you think about the needs for oral communication in life and in business, you will find that they are the same. These needs include:

1 Giving and receiving *instructions*
2 Giving and receiving *requests*
3 The *clarification* of details for accuracy
4 Negotiations requiring *diplomacy*
5 Situations where *assertiveness* is desirable
6 Personal and office situations where *bargaining* is taking place
7 The *introduction* of people, methods and ideas

Before examining each of these areas of speech, it should be pointed out that *listening* is just as important as speaking – or, to be more precise, it is the only real preparation for speech. It is always a more successful and pleasant conversation when people speak *with* each other rather than *at* each other. There are many other preparations before speaking and these will be examined, discussed and put into practice later, but listening is the prime factor in good spoken communication.

1   SPEECH FOR INSTRUCTION

When in a position where you are expected to give spoken instructions to an individual or a group, it is important to be aware of the following factors:

- Be certain that the instructions are of a type that can be given orally. Some instructions may be so long or so complex that putting them in writing would be more sensible and successful.
- Be certain that you express yourself clearly and in an appropriate manner, bearing in mind your listener's level of competence and understanding.
- Avoid any ambiguous instructions. Any instructions that are capable of being acted on in two different ways can lead easily to embarrassment or disaster.
- Speak carefully, at a suitable pace and in stages which reflect the stages of the particular process in which instruction is being given.
- Give your receiver opportunities to check back with you for verification of detail. Watch your receiver's face for signs of confusion. Ask, once the instruction has been given, if all of it has been understood.

Examples of spoken instructions

- 'We don't need any milk today, thanks.'
- 'Don't use the lift.'
- 'Leave two of the blue leaflets at all the houses on the left-hand side of the street, one of the red leaflets at the houses on the right-hand of the street and leave a white leaflet at every house with an even number.'

- 'When you have separated the paid bills from the unpaid, bring them to me.'
- 'When driving down a steep hill in icy weather you should try always to ensure that you are in a low enough gear to avoid having to brake too hard, as well as keeping a safe distance from vehicles in front of you and avoiding any large movements of your steering wheel. Otherwise a dangerous skid could develop which would be difficult to control in the prevailing road conditions.'

'Did I say coffee? I meant tea.'

- 'Please bring me the files for Warburton, French, Roberts and Dodd, as well as any information we have on their attendance over the last year. I also need a copy of Tuesday's *Financial Times* as it has a good article on export subsidies. I'd also like a cup of coffee if you've got the time – two sugars and no milk.'

EXERCISE

With a partner read these instructions aloud. Discuss the faults in each (unless you believe the instructions to be faultless!). Decide how the instructions could be improved. In the light of your discussion rewrite the spoken instructions to show how they could be better expressed.

COMMENT

I hope that in your discussion of the six examples of spoken instruction you noted the following:

a   Not all the instructions need rephrasing

b   Ambiguity featured in one of the instructions

c   Not all the instructions were expressed in appropriately staged sections when the instruction was complex

d   Opportunity was not always given when needed for the receiver of the message to check on details

2   SPEECH FOR REQUEST

We are constantly in situations in life and work where requests have to be made. We have been making requests since we were able to speak and it is easy to forget some rather obvious but important points that need to be considered:

1   When making a request we are giving work to someone and should be aware of this in the politeness with which we express our need.

2   The person to whom we are making a request may not be totally familiar with the subject of the request and so we should choose clear and simple language of expression.

3   There should be no ambiguity in the request made or the desired result may not be achieved.

4   In some cases it may be desirable to explain the purpose of your request. This is not simply a matter of courtesy, as some background information may well help the receiver to respond to your request more efficiently.

Examples of spoken requests

- 'I'd like the day off work tomorrow.'
- 'Could you shut the door, please?'
- 'Would someone please help me with this application form?'
- 'I need some background information on drawing up student profiles. Can you get me something suitable, please?'
- 'When the candidates have finished their essays, would you bring them to my office?'
- 'Please make sure that you get someone to check the foreword, index and dedication in the page proofs as well as the accompanying roughs for the cover illustration and then check these against the original proposal synopsis.'

EXERCISE

Discuss with a partner which of these spoken requests need rephrasing for better results to be achieved. When you have isolated the faults, rewrite the requests in a more suitable form. Compare the original with your version and check that no further improvements are needed.

COMMENT

a   The first request was not bad except that it should have offered an explanation of the reason for the request. This would have been both more polite and also have allowed the person to whom the request was made to judge the merits of the case.

b No alteration required (unless there were a number of open doors to choose from!).

c Not too bad except that a more specific request would have been likelier to get a positive reaction.

d A very vague request. 'Some background information' and 'something suitable' are very unclear and lacking in helpful detail.

e Ambiguous! Is it the essays or the candidates or both that are required to be brought to the office?

f It is to be hoped that the receiver of this request is familiar with publishing jargon or they will be rather bewildered. Let us hope that the receiver asked for further clarification if the details were not understood!

3 SPEECH FOR CLARIFICATION AND ACCURACY

Tom: 'I'll see you in town tonight then.'
Stan: 'Seven-thirty OK?'
Tom: 'Make it eight. Outside the Plaza?'
Stan: 'Suits me.'

The above exchange of dialogue may not win any prizes for drama or entertainment but it is an example of simple speech used for clarification of detail and accuracy of arrangement. If the opening line had not been expanded in the following brief discussion, Tom and Stan would probably still be wandering round the city centre looking for each other. Time and place were accepted or bargained for until a firm arrangement was definitely made.

In the world of work there are often more difficult areas of fact, decision and agreement that need to be settled in speech. The same principles as shown in Tom and Stan's dialogue are called for, however.

1 An unclear or unspecific statement is expanded by the partner in the exchange in order to aim for greater accuracy or clarity (*'Seven-thirty'*).

2 A check is made to see whether the new detail is what was originally intended ('OK?').

3 A further adjustment to detail is made by the original speaker in order to assure the partner that they both understand the arrangement or detail ('Make it eight.'). The adjustment may not be required, in which case confirmation of the detail should be made.

4 If there is still significant detail missing, then another adjustment should be made ('Outside the Plaza?').

5 A final check is made that the new detail is satisfactory or correct. (The question mark indicating a query in the tone after 'Plaza' checks and the response 'Suits me.' confirms.)

In other words, careful checking of detail on the part of both speakers leads to eventual clarity. Of course, if Tom had thought carefully before speaking he could have saved the need for the different stages of negotiation, eg:

Tom: 'See you at eight outside the Plaza?'
Stan: 'Suits me.'

Note that the check still has to be made by Tom, and Stan's confirmation has to be received.

EXERCISE

With a number of different partners, act out the following speech situations:

1 Discuss the important details for the arrangement of a surprise party for a person known to you and your partner.

2   Arrange to spend a day out somewhere outside your local area next weekend.

3   Discuss the necessary details for the invitation of a visiting speaker to your class to talk about some topic in your syllabus.

4   Arrange an outline programme of revision where you take it in turns to help each other at each other's house in the evenings for a week.

5   Arrange to meet in town one evening in the coming week to go to a film which you both wish to see.

6   Imagine your teacher is retiring. Discuss arrangements for making a collection and buying an appropriate farewell gift.

COMMENT

As in many of the exercises, the use of a tape recorder will be helpful. Once you have recorded your various discussions and arrangements on tape, review the results with a third party or the group as a whole. Check whether by the end of the individual conversation all necessary details have been clearly and unambiguously settled. List the faults that emerge from the criticism and discuss how they could have been avoided.

4   SPEECH FOR DIPLOMACY

You do not have to be employed in a top job in an embassy to require skills of diplomacy when speaking with people. The following down-to-earth situations all require diplomatic language to avoid 'painful' consequences:

● You arrive home at night an hour later than the 'deadline' given by your parents

- You forget to send your best friend a birthday card
- You are stopped by the police for exceeding the speed limit in a built-up area
- You have failed to produce an assignment for a teacher who is already dissatisfied with your progress

The list could go on and on. It is clear that, in everyday work or leisure, life is filled with potential situations where diplomatic speech can be very valuable in avoiding the worst consequences of one's actions. The above examples are *defensive* situations where you may be trying to defend yourself by language.

There are other occasions when you are actively using diplomatic language to try to gain something that you need or desire:

- You need to borrow a sum of money in order to go on a holiday with some friends
- You want to use your house for an all-night party and require your parents' approval

These two examples will remind you of the daily needs we have for diplomacy in our dealings with people around us.

EXERCISE

Use the following situations as the basis for a series of role play exercises with a partner or a number of partners:

1 Take it in turns to discuss some unattractive or annoying aspect of the behaviour or personality of a boyfriend or girlfriend. Your partner plays the role of the boyfriend/girlfriend. Discuss these defects in such a way that neither is offended. Choose language that does not hurt and which is inoffensive.

2 Take it in turn to try to borrow £20 from each other. The partner should aim to refuse tactfully and you should aim to get your way without bullying or resorting to emotional blackmail. After a stalemate has been reached exchange roles and start again.

3 Think of some particularly unattractive task and try to persuade your partner that it would be a good idea to help you with the task or even to do the task for you.

4 You have a long-standing arrangement to attend an event or go out with your partner. Explain to the partner that you wish to break the arrangement and not be committed in future.

5 Comment on each other's hair-style/dress/appearance in such a way that you try to persuade each other that a change would be for the better even though there is nothing wrong with the current style.

COMMENT

You will find that tone of voice, expression and careful choice of words are essential ingredients in order to be truly diplomatic in your conversations. Ideally, in each case neither party in the exchanges will be conscious of being manipulated, nor will either feel hurt or insulted. After each conversation you should discuss with each other what you were trying to achieve and what were the areas of greatest difficulty.

You will probably find that consciously or unconsciously you were using *euphemisms*. These are words or phrases that we use as substitutes for rather harsher realities. Overweight people for example always prefer to hear phrases such as 'well-built' or 'chubby' from others who refer to their size. Estate agents might refer to a particularly cramped house that they are trying to sell as 'compact' or 'easily managed'. Euphemisms are kinder or milder ways of referring to reality.

EXERCISE

Think of euphemisms that you have heard used for the following.

Write down as many as you can and then compare lists with
someone else in your class.

short	death	cheap	slum
ugly	toilet	old	cripple
boring	drunk	unemployed	mad

Remember that a euphemism is a milder or kinder way of saying
something. Make sure that your list does not contain words that
are more abusive than the original!

5 SPEECH FOR ASSERTIVENESS

A later section in the book will deal with the problems and techniques
of assertiveness but some preliminary definition and practice would be
useful here.

Assertiveness is an attitude of mind that is expressed in speech by:

- honesty
- determination
- persistence
- patience

Assertiveness should *not* be confused with:

- aggression
- sarcasm
- militancy
- bullying

Situations in homework and leisure life that are best resolved by the
adoption of an assertive attitude and manner of speaking might
include:

- Standing up for one's rights
- Putting a stop to behaviour on the part of a colleague or superior
  which you do not like
- Dealing with harassment
- Making someone else see your point of view

In general terms, techniques that can be adopted in situations where
assertiveness is required are:

- To avoid raising your voice, which suggests that you have become emotional and irrational
- Quiet but determined insistence by repetition of the case you believe to be right
- Acknowledging those parts of your opponent's case that are right but then stating your own case (such acknowledgement can be disarming and has the effect of impressing with your fairness)
- To avoid anxiety and feelings of guilt by fully justifying your argument

EXERCISE

With a partner take turns playing the following roles in the situations outlined:

1 You have bought a pair of shoes from a shop and, one month later, find that they have begun to fall apart. Take it in turns to be assertive customer and awkward shop assistant.

2 You are upset at a colleague's persistent smoking in the office. You wish to avoid secondary inhalation. Take it in turns to be complainant and determined smoker.

3 A member of the office staff or a student in your class is often telling racist jokes. You feel offended. Persuade this 'joker' that this type of humour is not required. Take it in turns to be offending colleague/student and complainant.

4 Your manager has asked you to buy a box of chocolates for his wife's birthday in your lunch hour because he is very busy. You feel you are busy too. Take it in turns to play busy manager and busy secretary.

5 You are the only one at home/in the office who does washing up, tidying, etc. You feel it is time you asserted yourself. Take it in turns to assert your rights.

6 The manager comes into the office and asks you to make him/her a coffee. This is not part of your job description and you are very busy. Take it in turns to 'resist and insist' in the coffee debate.

7 A married colleague keeps pestering you at work about meeting for a drink outside working hours. You don't feel comfortable with this harassment. Take it in turns with a suitable partner to settle the problem amicably but firmly.

8 You are on holiday and the room allocated to you in the hotel does not conform to the package holiday brochure's description. Explain to the courier representative of the firm that you do not want this room nor are you interested in settling for second best now or the promise of a refund later.

9 A friend owes you money. It is well past the date agreed for repayment. You have already dropped a friendly hint but this does not seem to have worked. Make sure you get your money back. Your partner will try to extend the loan.

10 A rather determined shopper has taken a place ahead of you in a queue. You are in a hurry and resent this kind of behaviour anyway. Establish your original position in the queue. Your partner will do his/her best to keep the position. No physical persuasion is allowed!

COMMENT

A third person observing your conversations can be of great assistance in analysing faults and weaknesses as well as strengths in your attempts to be assertive rather than emotional and aggressive. Discuss with your partner and observer any difficulties you experienced and where you felt uncomfortable in persisting with your point of view.

6 SPEECH FOR BARGAINING

In the home, at leisure and at work we are constantly in situations where some form of bargaining is taking place. Such discussions may be extremely informal (deciding who is going to wash up) or of great significance (deciding on nuclear missile withdrawal). Upon our success as bargainers can depend our personal comfort or the fate of nations. Whichever scale of bargaining you are involved in, the basic rules of conduct remain the same:

- Be sure of your facts
- Understand the other party's point of view
- Adopt appropriate assertiveness techniques
- Avoid confrontations and ultimatums
- Use a tone of voice and register of language suited to the situation

The reasons for the above criteria may seem obvious but some brief explanation should be of assistance in putting the rules into effective practice.

1   Being sure of your facts is essential as it is impossible to bargain successfully if your opponent has information that undermines your case. (It is no use claiming that your brother never does the washing up if he can refer you to the undisputed fact that he did it last night!)

2   Understanding the other person's point of view is not only reasonable behaviour but more likely to lead to success. If your opponent is aware of your understanding of his case by odd remarks you make, then there is less likely to be resistance against you getting your desired result. (Explaining to your manager that you know it is not usual for him as a busy executive to undertake work more commonly associated with junior staff *may* enable him to capitulate more easily!)

3   The adoption of some of the assertiveness techniques previously outlined can do your case no harm. Persistence, patience, etc, are ideal approaches to bargaining and diplomacy.

4 Confrontations from which you cannot withdraw without losing face are definitely to be avoided. It is no use setting deadlines or making threats that are unreasonable and incapable of being put into effect. This can be counter-productive and only leads to the strengthening of your opponent's position. (Your office colleague is not going to be over-impressed by threatening never to speak to him again for the rest of his life if he doesn't stop smoking. He knows very well that this is unlikely to be put into effect and he wouldn't be too worried if it were!)

5 The tone of voice in which you bargain should be calm and reasonable, rather than aggressive on the one hand or meek on the other. The register of your language should also be appropriately selected. It is easy to get tongue-tied and out of control of the discussion if you have become irate and are using language of an inappropriate register.

Register

This term refers to the 'levels' of language available at any time for expression of written or spoken communication. The following model will help you to see what is meant by register.

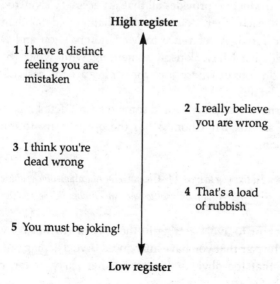

High register

1 I have a distinct
feeling you are
mistaken

2 I really believe
you are wrong

3 I think you're
dead wrong

4 That's a load
of rubbish

5 You must be joking!

Low register

You will be aware from the above examples that in everyday speech we select, consciously or sub-consciously, which point on the register of choice is best suited to our position. The choice may be dictated by the status or the age of the person to whom we are speaking, our familiarity with the person or the circumstances of the conversation. Being interviewed for an important job, you would probably adopt a different point on the general register of language to that used to chat to a good friend.

7   SPEECH FOR INTRODUCTION OF PEOPLE AND IDEAS

Whether it is for introduction of yourself, introduction of people to each other or introduction of your ideas on a topic, careful and coherent expression of information is essential. The introduction of people to each other with yourself as the 'go-between' is easy enough:

'Mr Jenkinson I'd like you to meet Mr Chomba. Mr Chomba is the education attaché at the Zambian High Commission here in London.'

Such an introduction provides all that is necessary to introduce two strangers to each other. You will notice that more detail than just the names is offered. A reference to Mr Chomba's job and where he works will give Mr Jenkinson something with which to start a conversation. Jobs or where you work or live are the basis of so much initial 'small talk'.

An alternative might be to add some relevant detail relating to Mr Jenkinson so that Mr Chomba has the opportunity to initiate the conversation.

'Mr Jenkinson I'd like you to meet Mr Chomba, the education attaché at the Zambian High Commission. Mr Jenkinson used to teach in Zambia in the 1970s.'

It is important to avoid getting in the way of further conversation between the pair that you have introduced. Avoid adding phrases and sentences that too obviously prompt either party. It can have the opposite effect to that intended when remarks such as the following are made:

'I'm sure you've got so much to talk about.'
'You have an awful lot in common.'
'I know that you're going to get along like a house on fire.'

Such remarks put pressure on the parties which often has an inhibiting effect.

The introduction of yourself or the introduction of your ideas on a topic are both situations that frequently arise in an interview situation. It may seem strange but talking about yourself and your experience can be very off-putting. There seems to be no obvious reason for this as you and your experience should both be very familiar to you! Perhaps this is the root of the trouble. *Because* you know so much about such a topic, you take too much for granted. Let us examine how best to present ourself and our ideas in an interview.

Introducing yourself

Sandra Chung has just come in to be interviewed.

'Good morning Miss Chung. Tell us a little about yourself.'
'Good morning. Well ... my name is Sandra Chung ...'
'Yes?'
'I'm eighteen years old ...'
'Yes?'
'I like reading and ... and listening to music.'
'I see.'
'What sort of things do you want to know?'

This is *not* a very good start to an interview. Sandra has not prepared herself, or does not realise the purpose of the interview. Sandra has forgotten:

a The purpose behind such an open question as 'Tell us a little about yourself'.

b   That she is being given the opportunity to speak coherently and to the point.

c   That her application form with relevant details is probably in front of the interviewer as she speaks.

d   That it is the way in which she speaks that is being judged rather than what she is saying at this stage of the interview.

'Tell us a little about yourself.'

Sandra is not playing the 'interview game' very well. This is because she is not aware of **a** to **d** above.

Although her application form containing her qualifications, experience and so on is probably in front of the interviewer, she should feel free to give a brief summary of the more relevant points in order to provide information about herself and her suitability to the position for which she is being interviewed. The interviewer is giving her an opportunity to show her ability to speak fluently and with relevance.

Sandra could have been given the opportunity to speak on the weather or her favourite sort of holiday, as it is primarily her ability to express herself that is being judged. The interviewer simply thought that she would be most at home speaking about a subject which she has at her fingertips – herself.

Given that versions or variations on this sort of question very frequently occur at interview, it should not be difficult to prepare a personal 'paragraph' or so of relevant information. Perhaps if Sandra had been prepared she might have responded as follows:

'Good morning Miss Chung. Tell us a little about yourself.'

'Good morning. My name is Sandra Chung, as you know. I'm eighteen and just finishing a BTEC course at Glasburn College. I've enjoyed the course very much, especially my placing with a travel agency on the work experience section of the course. While at college I took the opportunity to improve my typing skills and also attended a course on word processing. I hope to make my career in a service industry and I'm particularly keen to have an opportunity to further my interest in travel and tourism. I enjoy meeting people and in my spare time act as a volunteer assistant in a local old people's home.'

Information such as this will give the interviewer or interview panel an opportunity to pursue further questions based on the facts that Sandra has offered. Sandra has shown herself to be lively, involved and cheerful. She has also set the 'agenda' for the next questions, which should make the opening minutes of the interview less stressful.

EXERCISE

Make notes for an informal introduction of yourself like Sandra Chung's opening remarks at the interview in the example which you have just read. Try to jot down enough material for about a minute of easy and fluent speech. Do not write down a word-for-word script – just the bare bones of essential points that will serve to introduce your interests and abilities. Having got your remarks in a presentable order, take it in turns with a partner to make your introductory 'address' to each other.

Discuss how each of your introductions could be improved. In the light of your mutual criticism have another go at presenting your opening remarks.

Introduction of your ideas on a topic

Apart from statements of fact, an interview is very likely to require you to present your ideas on a topic. Nobody is trying to catch you out. You will not be asked to present a foolproof solution to some impossible task such as the Middle East crisis or the Northern Ireland problem. The subject will be one with which you are familiar – probably based on the course or training that you have recently undergone. A typical request for your ideas may be presented in the following form:

'Tell us about the strengths and weaknesses of the course of study you have recently completed.'
or
'Give us a brief outline of the main areas of your course and any ideas you may have concerning how the organisation or content of the course could be improved.'

This type of question can easily catch out a candidate. It should *not* catch you out as it is based on something that has occupied your time for the length of your course. No doubt you will have voiced your opinion several times during the course as to any weaknesses or anything wrong with it, and your ideas on how the course could be improved.

In order to make a reasonable attempt at answering such a question you will have to stay calm, remember the main areas of study and outline these to your interviewer. In order to offer ideas on how the course could be improved or particular areas of weakness within the course, you will have to be honest and recall particular areas of difficulty or boredom encountered by yourself and your group colleagues. Any areas of difficulty you experienced could lead you to remark that you wish more time had been allocated to this topic on the timetable or syllabus. Any areas of boredom may lead to the remark that such parts of the course had more time allocated to them than was justified. You will have to be prepared to deal with further questions or challenges that might come from the interviewer concerning these issues.

Incidentally the two questions that have just been suggested are *not* an invitation to have a long 'moan' about particular teachers or the lack of facilities at your school or college. They are questions relating to the course itself – a course that will have been studied all over the country.

EXERCISE

Since the interviewer who asks either of the questions previously outlined is offering you the chance to expound for two or three minutes without interruption, it is obvious that you will have to be reasonably prepared. As in the previous exercise, make skeleton notes outlining the main areas of the syllabus for your particular course. Underline or otherwise mark your notes where in your opinion there are particular strengths or weaknesses or areas requiring improvement. Jot down any remarks you might make to this effect during your two- or three-minute offering.

Without these notes, but with a partner as interviewer or audience, give a clear account in answer to either of the posed questions. Get your partner to time you and to make notes of any particular points worth criticism. You may be surprised how long three minutes actually is!

GENERAL SKILL EXERCISES

These are tests and exercises intended to help you develop your oral skills and gain increased confidence in your ability to express yourself. They are not necessarily connected with school, college or business. The exercises are designed to allow you to polish general oral skills that can then be applied to a work situation.

1 The running commentary

A commentary on an event that is taking place puts great demands on vocabulary and coordination as well as breath control. Sporting events are particularly difficult to give a commentary on as the pace and unexpectedness of events can easily leave you breathless and tongue-tied. By contrast an event such as the state opening of parliament is relatively easy as there is a very deliberate and well-prepared pattern to events.

If possible, make a tape recording of the group's commentaries and compare results.

a Give a running commentary on a classroom event or demonstration. The object of this exercise is to comment on the actions being carried out by a colleague in the classroom. The actions being carried out need not be elaborate. Even coming in the door, walking to a desk and sitting down can be described in fair detail. A demonstration such as cleaning a pair of shoes or styling someone's hair gives even more scope for commentary. Changes in pace and manner on the part of the demonstrator should all be reflected in the commentary.

b Turn down the sound on a sports event on television or video and take it in turns to provide a running commentary on the game or race. Each commentator should have thirty seconds and be followed without pause by the next person whose turn it is. As a variation a teacher could pick commentators at random. You do not have to proceed at the pace of a horse-race commentator in the final furlong but neither should you allow the pictures to speak for themselves. The idea is to treat the events on the screen as if they were reality and then by your commentary to try to recreate reality for an imaginary radio audience. As a rule it is unusual to let more than three seconds of silence go by for a radio audience or they will start thinking there has been a break in transmission. Speak fluently.

The skills of fluency and quick thinking and the extension of vocabulary are all developed by practice in running commentaries.

2 Prepared and spontaneous criticism

We are all critics by nature. Even as babies we are able to distinguish between what we like and what we dislike. As babies we are incapable of articulating in words the reasons for our loves and hates. We either gurgle with delight or cry in rage. As mature, reasoning people we can put words and reasons to our preferences and do so every time we discuss a television programme, a new record release, somebody's recently purchased shoes, a choice of car, etc.

a Prepared criticism: Agree with the group or a smaller number of people to watch a particular television programme. When you have watched it, possibly making brief written notes as you did so, prepare a criticism of the programme for presentation to the class or group as soon as possible after the programme's transmission. If you find that the morning newspapers have criticised the programme in their TV review pages, then take those along to the class with you.

When different people have presented their oral reviews to the group, a discussion can take place in which the views of the professional newspaper critics may also be aired.

Alternatives to television criticism might include:

Reviewing a film seen at the cinema or on video
Reviewing a sporting event
Reviewing the refreshments provided by the school/college canteen
Reviewing an advertisement
Reviewing a piece of music
Reviewing the course you are on or have been on
Reviewing the leisure facilities provided in your local area

Remember that criticism involves commenting on the good as well as the bad points, a certain amount of description, and suggestions on how improvements might be made, as well as the overall effect on you.

b Spontaneous criticism: This is similar to the above except that there is no time for carefully prepared notes. The object of criticism is presented to the group in the classroom itself. This might involve use of a video recording, a sound recording, a newspaper cutting or a visual display. It is up to the imagination of the teacher or individuals within the group to decide what is the object for criticism that is presented.

Having had a set amount of time to form an opinion on the object for criticism, individuals should present the rest of the group with a reasonably spontaneous review of their personal reaction. You should aim for at least two minutes of speech and, when several individuals have made their presentations, a group discussion can take place which gives a further chance to justify individual preferences.

Remember that you can learn from other people's criticisms (both of the object being reviewed and of your opinion). You will learn that there are many different opinions about everyday objects and events and that disagreement is not personal but healthy criticism. You will eventually learn the skill of speaking in a critical manner about something without notes and preparation.

3   Group discussion and reporting back

For this exercise the group should divide into smaller discussion groups of four or five people. The class as a whole is given an issue or topic to discuss and then disperses into smaller discussion groups for a quarter of an hour's debate and sharing of opinions on the topic.

A member of each discussion group is selected to give a report back to the whole class at the end of the quarter of an hour. The report should be of approximately two minutes' duration and may be given with the help of brief notes made during the discussion. These notes are only for reference and reminder. They should *not* be used as a script.

The teacher and group are quite capable of designing topics for discussion but the following may be useful starting points:

● 'Bad' language on television
● Discipline in the family

- Ideal holidays
- Homework
- The treatment of criminals by society
- The dangers of freedom
- The raising or lowering of the school leaving age
- The pleasures of being alone
- Work experience
- The ideal school or college

4 Individual reports

This exercise is designed to allow the individual speaker to gain confidence in addressing a group. The topics suggested can be adapted to the particular strengths and interests of individuals.

After some preparation each student take turns in addressing the group, without the use of notes, on one or more of the following topics:

a A perfect spot for leisure. With the help of maps, posters or photographs, recommend to the group a place with which you are familiar and which you believe to be a thoroughly good place to spend a holiday or take a break from the pressures of work.

b A good read. Recommend a book of fiction that you have enjoyed, give a brief outline of the plot and present a short sample of its content. (A passage with dialogue will help you to make the book 'come alive'.)

c 'This is how to do it.' Give a demonstration of some task with which you are familiar. This may be a hobby, a chore or something that you do at work. As you demonstrate, explain the techniques you are using in such a way that each of your audience can learn how to do it.

d A charity worth supporting. Explain the work of some charity with which you are familiar. Outline the policies, aims and objectives of the organisation. Explain the satisfaction you gain from being interested in the charity.

e A pet hate. Persuade the group why a particular hatred that you have for some aspect of behaviour is justified. You do not have to be deadly serious in your presentation, although the pet hate should be a genuine one.

5 Group concentration

With the group seated in such a way that there is at least three feet between individuals, take it in turns to pass a verbal message from the first person in the group to the last. It will work best if the group is seated in a circle as it is easier to arrange for new starters of the message.

The person whose turn it is to start the message writes down a message that has at least four significant details in it, eg 'Miss June Beardsworth will meet you at the corner of Albert Road and Park Crescent at 7.30 tomorrow night. She will be wearing a red coat and green shoes.'

In a voice that is only loud enough to be heard by the person sitting next to you, pass the message along the 'chain'. If the group has been listening attentively, the same message should emerge from the last person when it is checked against the written original. If there has been a lapse of concentration, this will not be the case! Listening can be just as important as speaking.

6 Individual concentration

With a partner chosen at random from within the group take it in turns to give detailed instructions for the completion of some task, which your partner follows to the letter as you go along. It is important for the giver of the instructions to be very precise and for the follower of the instructions to do only exactly what they are told. Even if the follower knows how to perform the particular task, he or she should do only what the instructor says.

Suitable tasks might include:

- Tying a pair of shoe laces
- Sowing a tray of seeds
- Wiring a three-pin plug
- Making a cup of tea
- Making a photocopy of an A4 page

7 Observation

Each individual within the group makes notes which describe a well known personality or another person within the group. The identity of the personally chosen 'target' is kept secret and it is up to the group to identify this person after a verbal description has been given (preferably without notes). Do *not* include in the description obvious details such as what the person in your group happens to be wearing. Limit your description to physical details and reference to mannerisms typical of the 'target'.

8 The essence of a place

Take it in turns to describe as vividly as possible a particular place with which you are very familiar. This might be a town, a building, a garden, a room, etc. Remember in describing the place to the group that we experience the world through *five* senses (sight, sound, taste, touch, smell). Your description of the place could benefit by reference to how the place concerned stimulates some of these senses. It should be more vivid if you 'use your senses'.

SECTION 2

The interview and appropriate preparation

An interview, whether it is part of your course or for a career, is of great importance to you. It is also the cause of much worry and heartache. This is probably because it is an unknown quantity and candidates are not sure how they can prepare for it. With a little thought it will be discovered that the interview need not hold such terrors. If we examine what the interviewer wants to get out of the interview and what the candidate needs to put in, we will soon arrive at a commonsense method of preparation.

1 WHAT THE INTERVIEWER IS LOOKING FOR

- What sort of personality does the candidate have?
- How likely is the candidate to get on with people?
- How does the candidate respond to pressure?
- How logical is the candidate?
- How honest is the candidate?
- Details concerning the candidate's strengths and weaknesses which are not apparent from the application form or letter of application
- How suitable is the candidate for the post offered?

What the candidate needs to show at interview

An awareness of the interviewer's requirements should give a candidate the basis on which to plan a suitable interview strategy. The following are essentials:

- To give an impression of a sensible and likeable personality
- To present yourself as a person who mixes well with people and a potentially useful member of a 'business team'
- To show that you are a person who reacts well under pressure
- To respond to questions and give details and opinions clearly and in a logical sequence
- To respond to questions with honesty but diplomacy
- To highlight areas of experience and training where particularly good results were achieved and explain honestly any weaker 'patches'
- To appear interested and knowledgeable about the post and organisation for which application has been made

2 PREPARATION

Much of the preparation for an interview takes place during your normal course of study. Knowledge of your subject and appropriate skills are always a strong base from which to launch your 'campaign' for successful interview. After all, the people whose names you have offered as referees will base their remarks mainly on your performance during your course. You will have been practising your skills of persuasive and logical speech in exercises during the year. It is up to you to reproduce your best under the stress of interview conditions.

Having said that, there are still individual preparations you can make in the period leading up to the interview:

Self-awareness

Practise being self-aware (which is different to self-conscious) by becoming accustomed to the sound of your own voice and noticing how posture and gesture in yourself and others speak for you. In the privacy of your own room practise introducing yourself to a mirror (preferably a full-length one). Notice your hands and feet and how

R.B.JACKSON

'Become aware of body language.'

distracting it can be if they are in constant movement as you talk.
Practise sitting in a position that is comfortable but don't sprawl. Give
a brief summary of your career so far to the person in the mirror.
Ensure that as you speak your hands are not straying self-consciously
to your face. Try to ensure that your expression and voice are friendly
and lively. Become aware of body language (see section 3 for a basic
explanation of body language).

Curriculum vitae

Write out a CV (curriculum vitae: a list of your personal and academic
details) to ensure that you can recall without strain any of the details
about which an interviewer is likely to enquire. Try to remember any
group activities with which you have been involved which will help
you to present yourself as a candidate who is likely to fit in well with
the team spirit of an office or business organisation. This might

include scouting/guiding, debating teams, quiz leagues, sports teams, amateur dramatic groups, school plays, ramblers groups, dance groups, music groups, choirs, etc. Interviewers are not so interested in your hobbies in their own right but to what extent they reflect a liking for people. There is nothing wrong with mentioning that you collect stamps or knit jumpers but these are not particularly gregarious occupations.

Do not forget any part-time or holiday jobs that you might have had. They may have little relevance to your application in terms of direct experience but they will show that you are used to the discipline of working in an organisation of some kind. Selling vegetables on a market stall may seem far removed from being an air hostess but it involves meeting the public and so would be of interest to the interviewer for an airline appointment.

Mock interviews

In order to practise keeping cool under pressure, work with a partner on one-to-one mock interviews. Take it in turns to be applicant and interviewer. The interviewer should make life as difficult as possible for the candidate, by interruptions, requests for repetitions, demands for further details, challenging of facts, etc. The candidate should aim to remain courteous and dignified under the interrogation which takes place. Since you will probably be much crueller to each other than a real interviewer ever would be, this practice will help you to develop composure under pressure.

A basis for this role-play exercise might be to select a number of job advertisements from a local or national newspaper and use these as the source material for the interview. Your own qualifications and experience will be real but you will have to slant it to the particular post for which your mock interview is intended. It is important that each of you takes the interview seriously and questions and answers are delivered in a realistic manner.

Just as an athlete would not dream of running in a competitive race without previously having run practice races in training, it seems obvious that a number of realistic role-played interviews are essential.

After all, there is more than a race at stake: your future career may depend upon the real interview.

Quick response

In order to rehearse the ability to think quickly before answering a question and also to think while you are speaking, there are a number of devices that can be used (they are games really). If we analyse the thought processes that go into answering a question, it becomes fairly clear that the mind needs to be incredibly active to deliver a useful response:

- We hear the question
- We interpret the question
- We decide what answers are possible
- We decide what answer is wisest in the circumstances
- We decide on what form and wording would be best
- We answer the question in the appropriate tone and manner

All this must take place in the space of about three seconds – or less! Impossible? Not at all. We do this every day. The only problem is that in the circumstances of an interview we sometimes seem to 'freeze'. Constant general practice in mock interviews with a variety of partners will help you when faced with the real thing to overcome this tendency to stall. Some of the following exercise-games will help to tune up your mental faculties and your speed of verbal response.

EXERCISES

1 Word association

A well known game in which the whole group can take part, although speed of reaction is tested better when a smaller number play. A word is taken as the starting point and then people take it in turns to respond with a word that bears some relationship to the previous one. A challenge can be made when it seems that there is no obvious connection and the person challenged must give a speedy and acceptable justification. If this is not given, then the person is out. The game continues until there is only one person (the winner) left. For example:

grass – green – golf – club – dance – guitar – Spain – holiday – beach – sea – sun – burn – fire, etc.

2 Going to the market
Another well known game in which the participants sit in a circle and build a sentence which grows longer and longer as the 'round' develops. For example:

First player: 'I went to the market and bought a banana.'
Second player: 'I went to the market and bought a banana and a pair of shoes.'
Third player: 'I went to the market and bought a banana, a pair of shoes and a jar of jam.'
Fourth player: 'I went to the market and bought a banana, a pair of shoes, a jar of jam and a fishing rod.'

This goes on until a player fails to remember an item in the growing list and is out. The list goes on until only one player remains. What is developed is attention to other people's words, memory and the power to think while speaking. You will find that with repeated practice you will be able to remember a considerable number of items purchased in the fictitious market.

3 The mayor's cat
A group exercise which is more demanding the larger the number of players. This depends upon knowledge of the alphabet and a reasonable vocabulary. The group sits in a circle and sets up a hand clapping rhythm.

First player: 'The mayor's cat is an awkward cat.'
Second player: 'The mayor's cat is a beautiful cat.'
Third player: 'The mayor's cat is a cuddly cat.'
Fourth player: 'The mayor's cat is a dependable cat.'
and so on.

The rhythm should not be too slow and a player is out on failing to provide a suitable adjective beginning with the appropriate letter of the alphabet and within the time set by the hand clap beat.

Players' ability to think ahead while others are speaking is tested as each is trying to calculate what letter of the alphabet is coming up and what adjective to supply.

4   Rivers – mountains – countries – cars

This is often played as a paper and pencil game but adapts well to oral testing. A large number of pieces of paper are prepared on which the words 'river', 'mountain', 'country' and 'car' are written separately. These pieces of paper are put into a box or other container. Some more pieces of paper are prepared which have the letters of the alphabet written on them. These are put into another box or container. A 'question master' is chosen who picks a piece of paper from each box and then demands of the player whose turn it is to play: river – letter D? The player then has two seconds to respond with 'Danube' or some other suitable answer. The question master should keep up a demanding pace and the players be obliged to think very quickly as well as answer correctly.

None of these games has a direct bearing on the interview but they encourage quickness of thought and dexterity of mind. They are all capable of being practised with a single partner as well as within a group.

Honesty and diplomacy

Responding honestly but with diplomacy to the demands made in an interview is most important. It is always a good idea to make a copy of any letter of application and CV that you submit for interview so that you can check back before the actual interview takes place. In this way you are unlikely to be caught out by reference to details that you had forgotten you had written.

Before the interview it is worth reading your application again and trying to imagine what weaknesses an outsider would discover. Go over these areas in your mind and work out how you could overcome or explain these weak 'patches' in your application. Do not be tempted to make excuses that blame your shortcomings on others. Criticism of teachers or institutions will not go down well with interviewers as they will interpret this as lack of loyalty and tact. Since loyalty, tact and diplomacy are qualities that an organisation will be looking for in its employees, it is clear why you should avoid 'passing the buck'.

Selling yourself

Finding the right balance between self-confidence and modesty is most important. It must be stressed that an interview is no place to be self-effacing. You are there to sell yourself and to do this you must appear confident and forceful without being brash and boastful. Timidity and lack of confidence are suggested by phrases such as:

'Well possibly'; 'I think that maybe'; 'Perhaps'; 'I can't be certain but'; 'I suppose that'; 'I could be wrong but'; 'Well maybe'.

To avoid prefacing your remarks with such phrases will be very much to your advantage.

There is nothing wrong with pausing before answering a question. On the contrary, the interviewer is likely to be impressed by your thoughtfulness – so long as the pause does not go on for too long, as this may be interpreted as indecision!

There is also nothing wrong with asking the interviewer to repeat a question or to clarify exactly what is being asked. This shows your desire for precision. Do not adopt this technique too often as it could be interpreted as stalling for time. Use your commonsense.

Your tone of voice, posture, eye contact and body language will all help to give the impression of a serious, confident candidate. Practice with a mirror and a critical partner will build up skills in this important area.

Make a list of possible 'open questions' and practise answering them in an appropriately confident manner.

Possible questions might include:

- 'Have you enjoyed your course of study?'

- 'What personal qualities do you feel fit you for the advertised post?'
- 'Where do you see yourself in five years' time?'
- 'Do you enjoy working with people?'
- 'What interests do you have outside the classroom?'
- 'What items currently in the news do you feel concerned about?'
- 'Why do you wish to join this particular company?'
- 'What sorts of things do you enjoy reading?'
- 'What kinds of holiday do you enjoy?'
- 'What sort of lessons have you learned from your part-time employment?'

Research

Researching the company or organisation to which you are applying is most important. If the business is a retailer or service company, go to a local branch and notice its layout and window display, make a note of any features that strike you as distinctive or unusual, talk to any of the staff who can spare you a moment of their time and find out what the company is like to work for.

If there is not a local branch or if the company is a manufacturer to whom it is difficult to get access, go to a local library and ask one of the assistants in the reference section to provide you with any directories and other publications that will give you details of the business concerned. Try to discover whether the business is growing in size, whether it has overseas offices or plants, what other companies are involved with it, etc. Try to find material that could form the basis of an intelligent question or two in the interview.

A question that candidates often seem to find difficulty with in interview is the apparently simple one that frequently comes towards the end, 'Is there anything that you would like to ask us?' Many candidates feel that, as this question comes towards the end of the interview, it is a signal to get ready to depart. Responses such as:

'No, I don't think so.'

or

'I can't think of anything, thank you.'

do not really get you or the interviewer very far.

You are being given the chance to take the initiative, to show your intelligence and keenness. If you have done a bit of background work there should be no shortage of intelligent questions to ask. Do *not* ask obvious questions, the answers to which have already been covered in the interview or in the job description. This will only suggest that you have not been listening or are rather unobservant.

Whatever question you *do* ask, listen to the answer that you get. There may be an opportunity or need to ask a supplementary question. It may be that your question causes the interviewer to ask you another question. Stay alert. This is your opportunity to leave a good final impression. If your opening to the interview was less than impressive, this is your last chance to compensate.

When it is quite clear that the interview is over, thank your interviewer/interviewers by name, shake hands and make a dignified exit. (Do not leave anything in the interview room. You will be thought scatter-brained and unimpressive if you have to go back to retrieve a briefcase!)

On the day

On the day of the interview itself follow these commonsense guidelines:

- Get up in good time. You do not need the stress of racing at the last minute for the deadline time.
- Ensure you know exactly where the interview is to take place and have some back-up transport arrangements made. If a relative or friend has arranged to take you by car, you can bet that this is the morning they will be ill or the car will not start.
- Wear something that is smart, comfortable and suitable and on which you decided the previous day. You do not need the stress of choosing your outfit on the day of the interview.
- If you normally have breakfast, then have breakfast; if you don't, then don't. Try to follow normal patterns on what will otherwise be an abnormal day.
- Check over your copy of your application and CV once more.

- Get to the place of the interview in good time, but not too early. You do not need the stress of rushing at the last minute nor do you want to have too much time for 'nerves' to upset you.
- Find an opportunity to check your appearance before you go in.
- Have a chat to other waiting candidates if the opportunity arises. This will distract you from your nerves and you may even pick up some useful information. You will certainly realise that others are feeling as nervous as you.
- Run over your CV again in your head.
- When invited into the room itself, breathe deeply, smile, remember to shake hands and *listen* to the names of anyone to whom you are introduced. Do not sit down until you are asked.

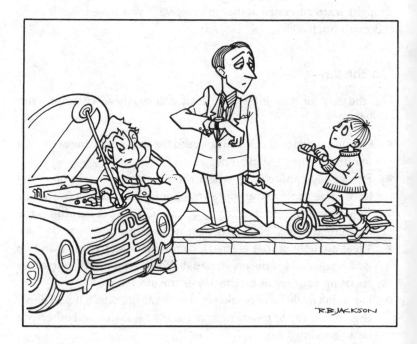

'Er – is that easy to ride?'

Listening and watching before speaking

Speaking with people whether at work, in an interview or in leisure time is not like making a speech. You are speaking *with* people, not *at* them. Speech is a two-way process which makes demands on both speaker and listener. This section will deal with the techniques to adopt when you are receiving speech. Only by adopting these techniques is it possible to offer speech effectively when it is your 'turn'.

'That was clever, wasn't it?'
On paper the above question is *either* straightforward and requests confirmation of the expertise of some act *or* is a sarcastic comment on some error or clumsiness. Only by *listening* carefully to the intonation and stress put on the words by the speaker and *watching* facial expression could the listener be certain what interpretation should be placed on the words.

'That *was* clever, *wasn't* it?' accompanied by a sneer would lead you to the assumption that there was distinct sarcasm in the air.
'That was *clever,* wasn't it?' delivered with an expression of enquiry could lead you to assume that your confirmation of a fact or opinion was genuinely being sought.

So much depends upon our awareness of tone, stress and expression in listening to the spoken word. Conversely the same applies when we are using the spoken words. Words can be tricky things.

1 LISTENING

It is most important that we listen with care when people are speaking to or with us. Inattention is discourteous anyway but can lead to mistakes, extra work and ill feeling. Life and work become much more tolerable when we communicate with care and attention. Conversations are more fluent, tasks easier and relationships more harmonious. Listening is as important as speaking – maybe more important.

Listening to tone

Words written on a page are much less flexible than words spoken by one person to another. On a page the meaning and message of the words are fairly fixed. When they are spoken we have to be aware of the different possibilities of interpretation. These possibilities arise, amongst other things, as a result of the tone of voice used by the speaker.

'We've only ten minutes.'

The above sentence seems fairly straightforward and the factual basis of the message will remain the same whatever the tone of the speaker. But the significance of the comment will vary tremendously dependent upon the tone of voice with which the words are spoken.

- **Lighthearted:** 'We've only ten minutes before this totally boring lecture is over – be cheerful.'
- **Worried:** 'Look, we've only ten minutes until the power goes off – we must finish the job.'
- **Persuasive:** 'We've only ten minutes till closing time – you may as well have a drink with me.'
- **Aggressive:** 'Can't you understand that we've only ten minutes? We've got to make it or all hell will break loose.'
- **Deliberate:** 'I've said it before and I'll say it again – we've only ten minutes to complete this section of the exam so we must be very careful.'

Obviously the context into which the phrase was put affected the interpretation of its significance. This was necessary because you were reading words on a page. In a real-life situation the circumstances would be understood and the phrase alone, delivered in a suitable tone of voice, would communicate all that was necessary.

EXERCISE

With a partner discuss and practise how the following phrases or sentences could be delivered in different tones of voice to convey messages of differing significance:

1 'Is that all you have to report?'
2 'There doesn't seem to be much alternative.'
3 'This could be your last opportunity.'
4 'I'm sorry – I can't do that.'
5 'Why did you go away?'
6 'Isn't there another way?'
7 'I can't believe that.'
8 'I think you'd better give me some details.'
9 'You can't go yet.'
10 'Why have you come back?'

At first you may feel a little self-conscious. Try to overcome this and to bring out the different shades of meaning that will be shown as a result of altering the tone of your voice.

Listening to stress

This topic does *not* refer to listening to a colleague discussing the problems of coping with a new job or the latest upset in the family! The stress referred to is the emphasis placed on a particular word or phrase in a sentence in order to bring out a shade of meaning. Altering the placing of stress in a sentence can considerably alter the message being given. It is important to listen carefully to where the stress is put if we are to interpret the message correctly. For example:

'I have asked the sales manager to come with us to the book fair.'
(He was not asked by anyone else.)

'I have asked the sales manager to come with us to the book fair.'
(It has already been done.)

'I have asked the sales manager to come with us to the book fair.'
(I haven't written to him.)

'I have asked the sales manager to come with us to the book fair.'
(Not the production manager.)

'I have asked the sales manager to come with us to the book fair.'
(Not the sales representative.)

'I have asked the sales manager to come with us to the book fair.'
(He may not be coming back with us.)

'I have asked the sales manager to come with us to the book fair.'
(To travel in the same vehicle.)

'I have asked the sales manager to come with us to the book fair.'
(Rather than with someone else.)

'I have asked the sales manager to come with us to the book fair.'
(Not the farm equipment fair.)

'I have asked the sales manager to come with us to the book fair.'
(Not the book sale.)

Try saying the above sentences, placing the stress on the underlined word. Listen to yourself and appreciate the subtle but important shifts in meaning and emphasis that take place.

Listening to what is really being said

There are a number of occasions when you should be aware that what is being spoken is not what is being said. That last remark is not as contradictory as it may sound! You will probably be able to recall times when you have spoken words that did not tell the whole story, for example:

'What do you think of this hair-style?'
'It's very ... interesting.'

The speaker is really replying that the hair-style is more than interesting; it is weird/bizarre/like nothing on earth/etc. This is not lying. It is use of euphemism for diplomacy. The person who made the enquiry will understand by the nature of the reply and the significant pause before the word 'interesting' that the hair-style is not a raving success. A code of language has been used that both people understand but which avoids confrontation.

We should listen carefully when people ask us questions or reply to us, to check that a code is not being used which makes the spoken words more significant than they seem to be on the surface.

EXERCISES

1 Decide what is *really* being said in the following sentences:

a 'The new filing system is very complex, isn't it?'
b 'The new assistant is rather quiet.'
c 'Mr Brown is very forthright in his views.'
d 'I find Indian food a little spicy for my taste.'
e 'You might like to check those figures again.'
f 'I've seen more accurate typing.'
g 'You do dress casually, don't you?'
h 'The film was ... unusual.'
i 'The class is rather boisterous on Friday afternoons.'
j 'Oh, he's always full of bright ideas.'

With the help of a classmate you can discuss whether these sentences mean different things to each of you. It will be easier to 'hear' the code if you speak the sentences aloud.

You will probably find in your discussion that what has caused the gap between surface and real meaning is the use of guarded or euphemistic phrases or the tone of voice that the word-stress causes you to adopt. Pauses between significant words can also cause a shift in interpretation.

2 With a partner take it in turns to play the following roles:

a Very polite employer who is trying to suggest to a new

employee that there are faults with effort, accuracy, punctuality, attitude and attendance. The employer does not want to reduce the new employee to tears but must try to bring about a change in performance. One of you should play the role of the employer who is using language 'in code' and the other should play the employee.

b A rather chauvinistic colleague who is being politely put in his place by someone who does not wish to bring about conflict but is quietly determined to make the person realise that his behaviour and attitude is personally unacceptable.

c A colleague at work or in class is getting into some rather bad habits and company. This person should be brought to recognise the dangers without causing a reaction against the subtle advice.

After each of these role-play sessions discuss whether the approach was too heavy-handed or too subtle. Decide how improvements might have been made to bring about the desired result.

2 OBSERVING UNCONSCIOUS MESSAGES

Another way of judging whether what is being spoken is entirely what it seems is to observe the way in which the words are delivered. The general term 'body language' is used to refer to those unconscious messages that a speaker often gives while speaking or listening. This is a complex subject but some of the more obvious aspects should be touched on so as to give a more complete picture of the communication process.

Rapid eye movement

We all blink as a matter of course but to some extent the rate at which we blink can give away the stress or tension that we are feeling. Blinking at a rate that is more rapid than normal suggests that we are unhappy with the situation or what is being said to us or demanded of us.

For instance, if a person is saying 'Yes, I'm pretty sure I understand that', but the eye blink rate is clearly more rapid than normal, then it is possible that you are not being told the entire truth, or that the person has been thinking about something else and not listening to you. Either way, it might indicate that running over the instructions or explanation again would be advisable – better safe than sorry!

A slow blink rate may indicate that a person is calm and in control of a situation, relaxed, at ease and comfortable. It is possible that the person is a good actor but such 'disguise' seldom extends to unconscious eye movement.

Repeated mannerism or gesture

We all have some physical mannerism or gesture that is a natural or unconscious part of our behaviour. When working with a group of people you will soon be aware of these individual idiosyncrasies. They may mean nothing at all. On the other hand an alteration in the pattern of these mannerisms may indicate tension or inability to cope with a situation. Typical mannerisms and gestures that you have probably observed in yourself or others might include: foot tapping, finger drumming, rubbing the chin, pulling an ear lobe, scratching the head, etc. If you have observed that the mannerism increases or alters when the individual is in a stressful situation, then you will be aware to watch out for this shift in pattern when they are dealing with you. In this case look for what the body is saying while the words are being spoken and whether both the received messages are the same. In other words – watch as well as listen.

Open posture – closed posture

The way we sit and stand is very often unconscious. Without an extensive range of photographs it is impossible to go into all the 'signals' we send regarding our mood, personality and state of mind. There are some general tendencies that are worth noting, however, which will help us to gain some indication of how the person with whom we are talking is feeling.

Open posture is recognised most easily in a seated person:

- The head will be level or even tilted slightly back at times
- The hands will be resting with palms open or loosely folded on the person's legs or on the arms of the chair
- The legs will be stretched out or loosely crossed
- The feet will be flat on the floor or casually crossed
- The general body posture will be vertical or relaxed

This usually indicates in the average person that the mood is calm and comfortable.

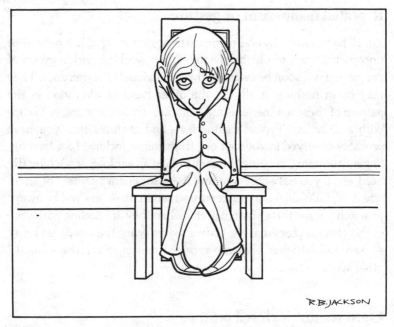

R.B.JACKSON

'Well, I've always been warm and outgoing ...'

Closed posture is characterised as follows:

- The head will be tilted slightly down from the level with eyes difficult to see

- The hands may be in a clenched position or hidden at the side of the body
- The legs may be tightly crossed or close together with knees touching
- The feet may be turned in with toes together but heels apart
- The general body posture will be hunched or rigidly vertical

This usually indicates in the average person that the mood is nervous and stressed.

Space occupied

When standing talking to someone we all adjust our position so that we are at a distance at which we feel 'comfortable'. This space between people varies between races and countries. Experts tell us that Americans, for example, are comfortable standing closer to each other than British people would be. We do not have to carry a tape measure round with us to check on this distance but we will be soon aware when a person stands noticeably further off than the average!

A person who seems at ease in the normal proximity between speakers is probably comfortable with what is being said. A person who keeps a distance greater than the average may well be worried by what is being said. If the distance varies during the conversation, it may indicate that the person is happier, or unhappier, with the progress of the conversation.

When we see a combination of all these factors it should give us a reasonably good idea of what is really happening in the communication process. For example:

Would we be really happy that we were communicating well and to our listener's satisfaction if we noticed that the person was standing about a foot further away than normal with feet turned toe in and rapidly blinking their eyes? They may be saying 'Yes' with their words but they are almost certainly saying 'No' with their body.

3   LISTENING TO AND UNDERSTANDING GIVEN INFORMATION

'There will be a fire drill tomorrow afternoon. It will be necessary to inform the teaching staff of this but not the students. If they have any problems they should contact the administrative office but not between 2.00 and 3.00 pm.'

If the above information was given to you, there is little doubt that you would have some difficulty in understanding what you were supposed to do in response. The faults in this attempt at communication are:

- ambiguity
- incompleteness
- lack of clarity
- poor structure

This is an example of the type of information that, if it had been written down, would have been checked and amended in the light of these faults. Too often when speaking we take insufficient care and do not give ourselves the time to correct our message mentally before giving it.

- **Ambiguity**   The ambiguity in this piece of spoken information lies in the pronoun 'they'. Does this refer to the teaching staff or the students?
- **Incompleteness**   What is the receiver of the information supposed to do? Should a memo be drafted? Should a notice be put up in the staffroom? Is somebody else going to inform the teaching staff?
- **Lack of clarity**   What sort of problems should be given to the administrative office? Does the inappropriate time refer to today or tomorrow?
- **Poor structure**   Although the message starts off with the main topic of information, it wanders off into imprecise additional information and does not conclude with an opportunity for the listener to check on the information.

If you were receiving information as imprecise as the example given, you would be well advised to ensure that the speaker did not get away before you had clarified the information. When receiving information by word of mouth it is always advisable to check it by one or more of the following methods:

1   Repeat the instructions or information to the speaker

2   Check on complicated or ambiguous information or details

3   Make notes where needed

4   Check on the context of the information – the background reasons for giving it

Repeating information

In the example of the fire drill information the receiver of the information might well repeat it as follows:

'That's a fire drill tomorrow afternoon and the teaching staff to be informed. Any problems to be communicated to the administrative office except between 2.00 and 3.00 pm.'

This repetition in summary form allows the listener to be sure that the information has been received correctly and enables the speaker to check that the right message has been given and that it has been understood. In other words repetition allows both giver and receiver of information to be sure that there is accuracy and comprehension of the information.

Checks on detail

When the information given contains details that might be significant or lead to confusion if errors were made in giving it, it is very important to check that you have received the information correctly. In the fire drill example a check such as the following might be made:

'So it's the teaching staff who should contact the administrative office with any problems but not between 2.00 and 3.00 pm? Is that hour today, tomorrow or both?'

Such a check will allow any ambiguity to be removed and both giver and receiver of information can be sure that it has been successfully communicated.

Making notes

Unless the information that is being given is very simple or obvious, the receiver would be well advised to make a rough note of the gist of the information to ensure that the message is remembered in general and in detail. The note would not be a word-for-word transcription but something like the following:

Fire drill tomorrow pm.
Inform staff but not students. Difficulties to admin office but not 2.00–3.00.

This note will allow the receiver to make checks, repeat information to the giver and have a record for later action.

Asking for context

Knowledge of the context to which the message refers often allows a more efficient follow up to the information as well as greater understanding. If you were told by your employer that he was considering buying a new word processor, it would be worth checking the background to this information (the context). If this was for his own use then you are not involved. If you are likely to be using the new machine then you need to know, as you might have some useful advice or knowledge in this field.

In the fire drill example a check on context would be:

'Is the fire drill being conducted by the college safety officer or the local fire brigade?'

This would allow you to judge the relative importance of the drill (although all fire drills are important) and to know of any special extra arrangements that might need to be made (such as arranging for an area of the car park to be kept clear for a fire engine).

Any or all of these methods should be used when receiving information, as the communication process is made more efficient. Since you will often be the giver of information as well as the receiver, an awareness of the checks that often have to be made should remind you to be clear, unambiguous and concise in your speech.

EXERCISE

In these role play situations you should take it in turn with a partner to give and receive information. The use of a tape recorder and/or third person as observer will allow analysis of how successful the giving and receiving of information has been. Both giver and receiver of information should bear in mind the suggestions made in this section for checks, repetition, etc. The situations given should allow a lot of flexibility in your choice and permit you to apply your own personal details.

1 Give relevant details of a book that might be useful for study or pleasure. In addition you may suggest where the book is available. (Do not just invent a title but base your role play on some facts you will have researched beforehand.)

2 Give a simple recipe and instructions for preparation. Do *not* simply memorise a passage from a cookery book, as an oral message is not just repetition of written information. (Be realistic in your choice of recipe as anything too complex would be passed on in written form.)

3 Inform your partner of a programme on television that you think would be useful to record on video. Make sure that the partner has all the relevant information to make a decision as to

whether the programme will be useful and also to make a recording at the appropriate time, etc.

4   Give details of the arrival and reception of an important visitor to your college or place of work. Give sufficient detail to allow your partner to make arrangements to receive the visitor or to inform others of the arrangements made.

5   Give your partner outline details of the syllabus for a particular course with which you are familiar. Assume your partner is considering taking up the course so that advice may also be included in the information.

6   Give the necessary information to enable someone to apply first aid in an 'accident at work' situation. Do not choose too complex an accident and ensure that the receiver is capable of dealing with such an accident. Your college or place of work will probably have a stated procedure for dealing with accidents in the workplace, so check this beforehand and include it with your information.

7   Give details of a person's name, address and telephone number. Although such information would normally be written, there are occasions in work when this type of information is given orally. You may, if you wish, add some details or instructions regarding writing or contacting the person whose details you have given.

8   Inform your partner of the advantages of a word processor over a typewriter. This information can refer to technical details but also should include general advantages in efficiency and accuracy. You may need to refer to your course notes or catalogues and other literature before attempting this role play.

4 LISTENING TO QUESTIONS AND REQUESTS

'How do you get from London to Paris cheaply?'
If you were asked such a question as part of your work, you would be quite justified in wondering what the questioner was talking about. With a little thought you will realise that the question has the following faults:

- It is incredibly imprecise. If one wanted to be facetious the answer could be that walking and swimming is the cheapest method. Clearly the questioner had something less energetic in mind!
- It lacks sufficient detail for any sort of answer to be formulated. Is a single person travelling? When is the journey due to take place? Is speed an essential element in the journey?
- There is no indication of the sort of detail the questioner requires in an answer. Is a simple response like 'train' required or are some financial estimates wanted as well?
- The question is put impolitely. If the receiver is required to do an amount of research in connection with the query, some sort of apology for the effort being demanded is desirable:

   'I'm sorry to put you to any trouble but ...',
or
   'Would you mind checking on ...'

These are both appropriate remarks with which to preface a query of this nature. There are, of course, many other similar phrases that could be used to show your gratitude for the information that is being requested.

If you are making requests or asking questions (or on the receiving end of such queries), the following factors should be noted. An awareness of these as a questioner and as a receiver should allow you to put your requests clearly and respond with efficiency.

Opening statement

An opening statement of your reason for making the request or asking the question can be politely expressed and allow the receiver to gain some idea of the context of the information required. In this way the person to whom the request is being made will be happier to make the effort demanded and more able to give accurate and relevant information.

In the poorly expressed example given at the beginning of this section an opening statement such as the following would be more appropriate:

'I wonder if you'd mind checking on something for me? I need to send my assistant to Paris from Heathrow this weekend. She will only be there for half a day but the budget is rather tight. Could you ...'

In this way the person who is expected to respond will feel less reluctant to have their time imposed upon and will also be in a better position to respond efficiently with the required information.

Avoidance of irrelevant detail

Although the poorly expressed example lacked detail, it is a common fault for questions to be asked which are lost in distracting irrelevancies. Although the speaker may feel that the details are interesting or of some use, very often they are counter-productive.

'I've got a favour to ask. Shirley Jones, who works in the research section, needs to get to Paris to a conference on methodology. She's working on a project for the international banking section. You probably met her at the last staff get-together when Johnson left. Anyway ...'

Although this may be cheerful and polite, it gets the listener nowhere. The only directly relevant reference so far has been to Paris. If this pace is sustained it will take a long time for the receiver to get a clue as to what is being requested. A combination of politeness and concisely expressed, relevant detail is what is required for successful communication and understanding of a request.

Organised structure

When a request is made or question asked which is in any way complex or in different parts, the sentence or sentences should be organised in a helpful and logical order. Although all the important details may be presented, communication will be hindered unless they are in the most effective order. The order may be chronological or in naturally-linked stages, depending on the subject matter.

A chronological sequence might be as follows:

'Could you find out the proportion of part-time and full-time employees and then give the figures to the personnel officer?'

A staged sequence might be:

'I'd be grateful if you could get me the sales figures for the last five years, the advertising and publicity files and then the company reports for 1987 and 1988.'

This will allow the receivers of the requests to make quick and accurate notes of the requirements and to react in an efficient manner.

Repetition check

As we discussed earlier in this section, once the request has been made or question asked it is often advisable for the receiver of the message to check that the details are correct. This is done by making a quick check with the speaker that everything has been correctly understood. Obviously this is efficient as well as assuring both parties that the communication has been accurately transmitted and received. A check on the example given in the last section might be as follows:

'That's five years' sales figures, files for advertising and publicity and company reports for '87 and '88? Anything else?'

The repetition check is simple but effective. Its use does not take up much time and is equally effective when on the telephone or when face to face.

EXERCISE

Put the advice given in this section into practice by role playing the following request situations with a partner and tape recorder or a third person as observer. Make sure that after each role play you discuss the strengths and weaknesses of the requests and responses. Where there is an obvious fault discuss improvements that are needed and repeat the request (perhaps with your partner taking the other role).

1 Ask your partner for a file or a textbook. Make sure that the partner has adequate information to allow the request to be undertaken successfully. Do not just leave the request as given and received – act upon it to ensure that the request has been practically and totally understood.

2 Ask your partner to go somewhere to meet someone or to carry a message to someone. The person making the request should ensure that the receiver of the request has understood *who* is to be met, *where* the person is to be found, *when* to go, *what* to say and, possibly, *why* this is important. It is equally important that the person receiving the request checks on these details if the message is less than totally clear.

3 Request the names and addresses of a small group of staff or students or local businesses. Be realistic in the number you request as anything above three or four would be presented in written form. The receiver should ensure that the requested details are already known so that a check may be quickly made on the accuracy of the resulting list.

4 Ask your partner for advice on a suitable leaving present for a member of staff. Make sure that the amount of available money is mentioned together with the expected date of the presentation.

5 Request directions for getting by car from your school, college or workplace to an address about a mile away. Make sure when making your request that you know the best route so that a check can be made.

6 Ask for advice on how to word a proposal at a committee meeting. Do not make the request a totally general enquiry but have an actual proposal in 'plain language' that you wish to have put into 'committee language'.

7 Request details of the academic background of an individual in the group as if they were being considered for a post in a business organisation. The receiver of the request should check that the requirements are understood and give the requested details to the questioner.

8 Ask for two telephone calls to be made which are intended to pass on a change in a timetable. The calls must be made in a particular order. Check that the receiver of the request has understood it. As a larger group activity you could develop this into an actual telephone exercise in which the details are passed on to third and fourth parties.

SECTION 4

Skill areas in oral communication

1 FORMULATING REQUESTS FOR SPECIAL PURPOSES

At school, college and at work it sometimes becomes necessary to make requests of colleagues that are particularly demanding or are being made of someone who is your superior in the organisation. It may well be that the two problems coincide and your 'favour' is also having to be demanded of the superior. Naturally such requests will be made politely and clearly, as was outlined in the previous sections. In the case of a special situation such as that just mentioned note that you should:

- Adopt a tone appropriate to the circumstances
- Make the request of suitable length
- Justify the request
- Choose the most suitable time to make the request
- Organise your request clearly and structure it sensibly

The following example shows how *not* to go about making a special request to a superior in the organisation.

Tony Arnfield had been learning to drive. He had spent a considerable sum of money on lessons. The travel agency for which he worked had allowed him the odd hour off work to fit in extra lessons. Tony was due to present a slide show and talk to a local group of senior citizens as part of a special promotion campaign for holidays for the

'I'm just going to the café over the road – won't be long.'

elderly. Two days before this talk was due to take place Tony received
notice that he could have a last-minute appointment for his driving
test because of an unexpected cancellation. His driving instructor told
Tony that he was ready for his test and the delay otherwise would be
three months. Tony decided that he must ask his employer, Mrs
Armitage, for permission to take his driving test instead of giving the
slide show and talk.

It was half an hour before closing time and a large delivery of the
next season's brochures had just arrived. Mrs Armitage was busily
checking off the brochures against her original order. A customer had
just come into the shop.

'I've just had the opportunity to fit my driving test in early due to
a cancellation, Mrs Armitage.'
'Really? That's nice for you, Tony.'
'It's Friday. It'll be OK, won't it?'

'Friday? You're doing that presentation at the community centre for the senior citizen's group, aren't you?'

'I can do that another time, can't I?'

'I'm afraid you cannot, Tony. I think I've been generous enough with time off, don't you?'

'I suppose so.'

The conversation finishes with resentment on both sides. Tony has to miss the chance for an early driving test and Mrs Armitage is left with a rather poor impression of Tony Arnfield.

What went wrong?

To put it mildly Tony made his request for a favour very badly indeed.

- He chose the wrong time. Mrs Armitage was busy with a lot on her mind. Although of some urgency there was no reason why Tony could not have waited until closing time before putting his request.
- His tone was inappropriate and lacked courtesy. He seems to have forgotten that he is asking Mrs Armitage to allow him more time off work as well as causing inconvenience and possible loss of business by putting the arranged presentation at risk.
- He has not tried to justify the request. If he had thought a little more before speaking he could have tried to convince Mrs Armitage that the business might benefit from his possession of a driving licence.
- The length of Tony's request is rather brief considering the extent of the favour he is asking. It is also somewhat rambling as he does not get immediately to the point. When the conversation has got round to the need for time off on Friday Tony puts the question in totally the wrong form ('It'll be OK, won't it?') and sounds both rude and presumptuous. The business may be a small one but he seems to have forgotten that Mrs Armitage is his employer.

EXERCISE

With a partner discuss how Tony might have approached Mrs Armitage in a better way. Role play how the conversation might have gone if Tony had made his approach more carefully and at a more opportune moment. Try taping the original dialogue and then your new version. Discuss how the improvements have come about.

It is hoped that much of the improvement is because you have paid attention to the following:

a Appropriate tone

When making a request of someone who is above or below you in the organisational hierarchy, or even your equal, it is essential that you adopt a balanced tone and manner in your speech and general attitude. It is too easy to go to one extreme or the other and be either fawning or forceful. Neither will be appreciated by any level of listener. You will not bully or beg your way into getting your request accepted. People will respect you more for a polite and honest statement of your needs.

b Suitable length

There is no mathematically precise length that can be put to the type of request we are considering. If the request is made too briefly you may be considered rather aggressive or presumptuous. If the request is long-winded then you risk being thought inefficient. Time, as they say in business, is money. Think about what you want to say and then say it in the most concise and polite way possible.

c Justification of request

It is important that you explain why it is of some importance that your favour is granted. If you can think of some way that benefit can ultimately be gained by the organisation or the individual by granting of your request, then so much the better. This is not an invitation to blackmail! Try to make your request seem reasonable in the circumstances. It is the circumstances that you are trying to explain.

d   Suitability of time

Try to ensure that you approach the person concerned at a convenient moment. Perhaps it would be possible to arrange with the person beforehand a convenient time during the day. You may be able to find out from a colleague or assistant when the person is likely to have a few minutes to spare. Choosing your moment can be quite important to the outcome of your request. Never put the person under pressure by asking for a decision at a few minutes' notice. It is easier for the person to say 'no' if a difficult request is being presented for immediate decision.

e   Organising your request

Be certain that you are in full possession of all the facts required by the person to whom the request is to be made in order to reach a decision. The details, the justification and the request should be presented in the most logical and most polite manner possible.

If we recall Tony Arnfield's unfortunate attempt to persuade Mrs Armitage to give him yet more time off for his driving test, he might have been better to make the following kind of approach:

'I hope it is not an inconvenient time to raise a small problem I have Mrs Armitage? I've been given a last-minute appointment for my driving test. It would be a real relief to be able to stop asking you for time off work for my driving lessons. Unfortunately the test is on Friday, just before I'm due to deliver the talk at the community centre. I would certainly like to have a driving licence as this would make me more useful as an employee. If it were possible to postpone the senior citizens' presentation, I wonder if you would consider letting me off?'

What else could Mrs Armitage do in the face of such a charming request but give Tony the time off and wish him luck?

GENERAL EXERCISES _____

Take it in turn to role play the following situations. Each involves making a rather difficult request of a person who is either junior, equal or superior to you. As usual, exchange roles and use a third person as observer and/or tape recorder for checking the successes and faults of your performances.

1 Request permission from the manager of the business to use the staff canteen as the site for a charity fund-raising fashion show. This would mean that the canteen would have to be closed in the afternoon of the day in question as preparations would be in progress. You might want to 'sweeten the pill' by suggesting that possibly free publicity would come to the company.

2 Request cooperation from a junior colleague to give up the allocated staff car-parking space for a week. A mobile blood transfusion unit will be parked in the space as part of a local campaign. This will probably mean having to take a chance on finding a space in the town in difficult street-parking conditions.

3 Try to persuade a colleague of equal status to go to the company resource centre and photocopy a few pages of a report for you because you are overloaded with work and in order to meet a deadline.

4 Make a request to your immediate superior in the department in which you work for permission to take a day off on the Friday immediately before the May bank holiday weekend. You need to travel to see a sick relative. You may wish to consider mentioning that this would be better than taking more days off at a less convenient time.

5 Ask a junior in your department at work to change shifts with you in order that you may visit a close friend who is in hospital. The shift you are offering is less attractive because of the unsocial hours but you really do want to visit your friend.

6 Persuade a colleague to go round the department at lunchtime taking up a collection for a national charity. You have got permission from the management for this to be done but you are being sent on a day's training session at the last minute.

7 Ask your course tutor for permission to be excused the holiday project as you are going on a skiing holiday with your old school. The work that has been set is important to your course so you will probably want to do it on your return but it will not be complete when the new term starts.

8 As a part-time hotel receptionist you realise that you have double-booked a room. Persuade the customer, who is now waiting to go up to the occupied room, that the alternative you can offer is almost as desirable although it does not have the sea view that was originally booked and is on the fourth floor instead of the first.

Make sure that you try consciously to follow the advice given at the beginning of this section. Practise until you find the tone, clarity and structure of your request easy to assume. You may be able to think of other similarly difficult situations to use as role play models.

2   EXPRESSING TABULAR/GRAPHIC DATA

In the world of work there may well be occasions when you are asked for information which exists in the form of lists or is expressed in graphs or other visual methods of presentation. Your job is to 'translate' this information into the required form of words. You need to be able to *interpret* the numerical/visual data very quickly, *select* the information demanded and then *express* the information clearly and concisely.

For example, a section manager approaches you and asks for an approximate figure for the Japanese and German motor industry's

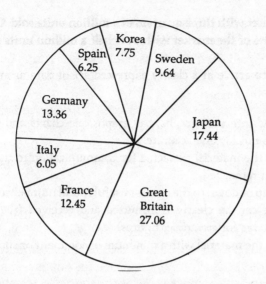

Fig 1 Motor industry's share of British market

share of the market in Britain. The computer terminal at your desk shows a pie chart as illustrated in Fig 1.

You also find on record the unit sales figures for the same period. Realising that the manager may require both percentage share and sales figures, you check this list also.

Sales for local and imported cars
(fleet and individual)

France	462 132	Japan	747 285
Germany	550 176	Korea	258 400
Great Britain	1 243 554	Spain	235 420
Italy	230 554	Sweden	321 207

With this information found, all that remains is to extract what is required and express it simply and efficiently to the original enquirer. In this case the response might be:

'I have the figures you require. Last year Japan had over 17% of the

British market with three quarters of a million units sold. Germany had over 13% of the market with over half a million units sold.'

In order to arrive at a clearly expressed set of data as above it is necessary to:

● Read and interpret graphs, bar graphs, pie charts and tables of statistics quickly and accurately
● Restrict the material extracted for communication to that which has been requested
● Round up or down to the nearest useful round number so that the message can be clearly transmitted and received (the original enquiry was for *approximate* figures)
● Express the material with a minimum of comment or superfluous detail

A bad or inefficient version of the statistics referred to might be expressed:

'Well I've got those figures you wanted. It took me ages to dig them out. The Japanese had 17.44 per cent of the market with sales of 747 285. That's a lot of cars! Germany sold 550 176 which was 13.36 per cent. It makes you think, doesn't it? Whatever happened to the British car industry?'

This is difficult to take in as a spoken response because the details are distracting and the irrelevant comment simply annoying.

EXERCISE

You may need to familiarise yourself with the interpretation of graphical and tabular data. Practice will be useful in interpreting and expressing selected statistics. You could gain experience by taking it in turn with a partner to ask for and research the following:

1   The rainfall figures for the area where you live in the months of

January and July and the equivalent figures for Torremelinos

2   The national expenditure in this country last year on education and defence

3   The rate of income tax currently deducted from top salary earners and average wage earners

4   The populations of London and New York

5   The cheapest fare locally available for a return flight from London to Paris and London to Montreal

6   The number of full-time students currently enrolled at your school or college and the number of full-time members of the teaching staff

7   The percentage of the population in this country who are of pensionable age and over, together with the percentage of the population who are in attendance at school

8   The average cost per hour of televising drama and sport

9   The average life expectancy in this country of a male and a female

10   The cost for an adult to travel both ways by train and by coach between two major cities.

These exercises are designed so that you will be able to familiarise yourself with a reference library and other local sources of information and statistics. You may find that you are having to ask for information either on the telephone or face to face as well as using written sources. You may be consulting librarians, local agencies, shopkeepers or members of college staff. Remember the factors that have already been discussed in the sections on 'listening to and understanding given information' and 'formulating requests for special purposes'. When you have researched as many of the answers as you can by actually using available sources, arrange to present your findings orally to your partner. He/she should then report back to you. (It will be interesting to see whether your answers are the same!)

3   DESCRIBING OR NARRATING

In work and especially in interviews you may find yourself asked to describe events relating to your training and experience as well as processes with which you are familiar. Although you may be totally skilled in these areas it is often difficult to describe the processes effectively.

If you have ever tried describing a very significant event to someone who has not experienced it, you will realise how frustrating this can be. To try to convey how marvellous (or disastrous) a party was to someone who did not go to it can be very demanding on your patience and your vocabulary. Here we are concerned with descriptions relating to the workplace and made for listeners familiar with the setting, so the process will not be so difficult.

The majority of this section will present techniques and exercises that are designed to allow you to improve your skills in the following:

- Selecting appropriate vocabulary for the particular topic
- Quickening your speed of verbal reaction in response to queries about a topic area
- Avoiding awkward silences that give an impression of incompetence
- Giving a 'performance' that seems naturally fluent

The exercises are adaptable and many are capable of being undertaken either solo, in pairs or within a group. In every case the use of a tape recorder would be an advantage in order to compare and contrast early and late attempts at the exercises as well as for constructive criticism of yourself and others.

Since these exercises are to assist you in choosing the right words at

'Tell Alice who is sitting by the window.'

the right time, it is best for you to assume that your audience is listening to a radio and you are giving a commentary. In this way there will be a concentration on the words and pressure put upon you to avoid too many silences.

You should aim for the following objectives in your responses to the exercises:

1 Avoid ambiguity – especially that which is caused by careless use of pronouns, eg:

'Tell Alice who is sitting by the window.'

Ambiguity can be distractingly amusing or even dangerous. In every case it momentarily distracts your listener from the main thrust of the description.

2 Avoid prolonged silences. Your listener will begin to suspect that you do not know what you are talking about. If you imagine the radio listener trying to cope with silence, perhaps wondering if the commentator is still there, then you will make more strenuous efforts to maintain a reasonable flow of narration/description.

3 Use helpful vocabulary that will present more than the bare bones of what is being described. Adjectives and adverbs that tell the listener more about objects and the way things are done help to achieve precision in a description, eg:

'The woman spoke to the man.'

This conveys a certain amount of basic information. A listener would be in a better position to understand the real picture if appropriate adjectives and adverbs were used, eg:

'The old woman spoke angrily to the young man.'
'The young woman spoke shyly to the older man.'

4 Incorporation of what is directly relevant in a description and the editing out of the distracting and irrelevant. You are probably aware that some people find it very difficult to filter the insignificant from the significant when giving a description. In attempting to tell us everything they end up giving us nothing but a blurred impression, eg:

'I met Jimmy Wilson the other day. I was just going to buy the evening paper to see whether my advert for the kettle I've been trying to sell had appeared when I saw him crossing the road by the greengrocer's shop. That's the shop near the library not that new one by the zebra crossing. He looked much the same as usual ...'

Assuming that the meeting with Jimmy Wilson is the significant part of the message, it seems to have taken some time already to get to the point. This example is only a slight exaggeration of the faults some people make in descriptive communication.

EXERCISES

The following exercises should be undertaken with a listening radio audience in mind so as to force a continued 'flow' of verbal description or narration. In many cases, however, the presence of a partner or group will be an advantage in building your confidence to speak to an audience. In other words you should assume the existence of a radio audience while 'performing' for a live audience.

1 Commentary on personal demonstration

For a partner or group give a demonstration of some skill or activity with which you are familiar. You should aim to give a physical demonstration, and at the same time describe what you are doing and why you are doing it. The activity should be something that is reasonably static and which allows you to speak while demonstrating. The following list of possible interests, hobbies and skills can serve as a starting point but you should certainly be able to extend the list to include your own interests:

- plaiting or styling hair
- repairing a bicycle inner tube
- grooming a dog or horse
- knitting or crocheting

- taking a photograph
- programming a video

- pruning a plant
- collecting and displaying stamps

Your aim should be to choose something from your work or leisure life that interests you or with which you are very familiar. Once the choice is made, decide what is most relevant and important to describe and prepare a three-minute demonstration/ commentary that can be delivered without written notes. You should be prepared for questions during and after your commentary to show that you can cope with the unexpected.

2 Commentary on partner's demonstration

The topics list can be the same as was used for the personal demonstration. The change is that you give a running commentary on what your partner is doing. You will need to see your partner's demonstration beforehand in order to prepare the outline of a suitable commentary for when it is presented to the group. You should aim to match your words of description to the varying lengths and speeds of the actions. In this way flexibility and variation in pace and detail of your description/commentary can be practised.

If, for example, your partner is demonstrating bread-making, there will be times when the action is quite rapid and other times when the process is slow and repetitive. You will need to react very quickly with words at the times of rapid action and 'fill in' with background information when the pace is less active. You should take your pace from your demonstrating partner rather than the reverse.

3   Unrehearsed commentary on another's actions
This type of exercise is similar to the last one, with the exception that there should be no opportunity for rehearsal or prior knowledge of what the other person is going to do. The range of activities for which you might be expected to provide a running commentary could include:

- A person entering a room, moving around the room, examining certain objects and then sitting down
- A person drawing something on a chalkboard
- A person giving a demonstration of some task (as in 2)
- A person in the street or grounds viewed through a window
- Any other situation that might give you the opportunity to make a spontaneous commentary

In making the above commentaries you should remember, as always, the need to describe clearly, vividly and with readiness for the unexpected.

4   Commentary on a group event (live or recorded)
This is an even more demanding exercise as you will have to try to deal with the complexities of a number of people taking part in

some group activity. Since the action and pace of the action will be in constant flux you must be prepared for variations in your own pace of delivery. You will also have your ability to edit out superfluous material tested, as not all the action will be significant.

Group events that might be a useful basis for commentary include:

- A tennis match
- A football match
- A concert or dance performance
- Any other event where you know the rules, background, etc

You will be able to think of suitable events for yourself after consultation with colleagues and teachers. Since the outdoor nature of many of the events may give practical problems in providing a running commentary, it could be more suitable to provide the commentary to a video recording of the event which can be played back with the sound turned down.

Whether you are providing a four- or five-minute running commentary live or to a recording, it would be helpful to tape record your commentary so that a check can be made later on the good and 'less good' aspects of your performance. A group of five or six students could pass the running commentary on from one to another after an agreed number of minutes and then play back the recording and compare the different performance techniques.

5   Personal commentaries for general practice

At times when there are no partners available or events for commentary are not immediately apparent it is good practice to provide running commentaries on your own domestic actions. Your family may think that you have gone mad and are talking to yourself but their comments should be ignored! For example:

'I'm getting up rather wearily and sitting on the edge of my bed. It's Monday and it's raining outside. Reaching rather stiffly for my slippers with the hole in the toes, I shuffle towards the bathroom to find it already occupied by my brother. I urge him to hurry up with a few well chosen words as I wait on the landing and watch the rain trickling down the panes of the window ...'

Remember that it is the *skills* that are important and which you are trying to develop through these exercises in oral communication. Although you are unlikely to be asked in work or at interview for a running commentary on bread-making or how you get up on Monday mornings, the skills of vivid and concise description which you have been developing through these exercises should be to your advantage.

4   PERSUADING PEOPLE TO YOUR POINT OF VIEW

In your college, work or leisure life situations arise when you need to be able to persuade someone to your point of view. This can apply whether you are in a position of some authority or someone is in a position of authority over you. In either case you need to possess skills of argument and persuasion to convince the other party concerned that your view in a matter is the correct one.

If you are in a position of authority over the person whom you wish to accept your point of view, it is *not* good policy to exert your 'rank' in order to get your own way. Unless you can convince people genuinely of the rightness of your case they will not be likely to respond effectively as they may still have doubts. If you are not in a position of authority but wish to convince someone of the validity of your case, it is *not* effective to adopt a 'cringing' tone as if you expected to have your request or suggestion automatically turned down. In other words a logical and balanced argument delivered in a persuasive and confident tone and manner is the most desirable approach.

The situations where the need to persuade someone (or a group of people) to your point of view might range from the domestic to the administrative. For example:

● You are deep into revision for some important examinations that are approaching. Normally you help out at home by washing up and doing some cleaning. You may wish to convince a parent or the whole family that you should be given 'time off' from your duties during the revision period.

- It could be that you are in employment and wish to convince the management of the advantages to be gained from going onto a flexitime working system.

In either of the above examples you would need to prepare your case carefully with full reasons and justifications for the change and be ready to argue your case logically and persuasively without emotional excesses in your behaviour.

Persuasive techniques

Apart from the general confidence that, it is hoped, is a part of your personality, there are a number of methods or techniques which are useful in persuading others:

a Choice of time

There are definitely times when it is unwise to approach people to give your point of view. You may be aware that there are times of the week when people are particularly busy. Since you want to be able to talk without the other party being distracted by imminent pressures of work or demands on their concentration, it may be a good idea to informally (or formally if the situation demands) request a time when it would be convenient to discuss a proposal.

b Plan your case

It is no use going into a discussion with some hazy, ill-defined idea of what you wish to achieve. You may find it useful to jot down on paper the advantages to be gained from adopting the change that you propose. It would be useful also to anticipate the arguments that might be raised against your ideas so as to prepare your counter-arguments.

Your preparation should be made in great detail so that there are as few unexpected reactions as possible during the actual discussion.

c Choice of vocabulary

Select words to state your case that are appropriate to the experience of the person to whom you are speaking. Jargon words are acceptable to a person who is familiar with the terms you may use but are only confusing and annoying to a person without similar experience. For example, to mention 'memory', 'ram', or 'disc drive' in a discussion with someone who is inexperienced with computers or word processors is not going to get you very far.

On the other hand you should not insult people by talking down to them as if they were slow-witted and needed everything explained in childish detail. If you assume that the target of your argument is reasonably intelligent but with slightly different experience to yourself, you should be able to judge the suitable vocabulary and register to use.

d   The rule of three

If you have ever listened to party political broadcasts or public speakers at large meetings, you may have noticed a trick of carefully timed repetition which is used to emphasise a point, eg:

> 'Never in the field of human conflict has *so much* been owed by *so many* to *so few*.'
> '*Unemployment is* soul destroying, *unemployment is* degrading and *unemployment is* unnecessary.'

It is worth considering exactly why such repetition is so often effective in implanting an idea firmly in a listener's mind. Presumably repeating something twice is insufficient to allow a pattern to form but repeating four times might run the risk of boring the listener or causing over-emphasis. The 'rule of three' is more likely to be of use when presenting a case formally than in an ongoing two-sided discussion, but you should be aware of its effectiveness.

e   Awareness of tone

As was suggested earlier in this section, it is important that you adopt the tone most appropriate to the situation. If you are trying to persuade a person with whom you are on close terms to agree with a proposal, you will probably use a different tone to that which you would use when persuading a superior with whom you are not close.

'Don't you think we've got to get something done about the terrible standard of the staff canteen, Tom?'

'I'd welcome an opportunity to discuss the possibility of streamlining the staff catering service, Mr Thompson.'

The more formal version of the above is not meant to sound 'posh' but is probably a more effective method of approaching a person in the organisation who might otherwise feel that he/she was being criticised for allowing the 'terrible standard' to have developed.

f The head rules the heart

Too often the person trying to persuade an individual or a group allows emotion to rule the expression of the case. It is very tempting to argue for something that you feel strongly about in a manner which is obviously guided by your strength of feeling rather than the strengths of the case itself. The display of emotion will perhaps convince a listener that you feel strongly about an issue but not that you are automatically right. For example:

'We've just got to get a grip on the amount of time wasted by staff using the telephone for private calls. It's absolutely ridiculous that hours are wasted by well paid staff gossiping for ages on our company telephones!'

The above emotional outpouring would certainly convince the listeners that there was a strongly felt desire on the part of the speaker to restrict the use of the telephones. The emotion is obvious but whether the members of staff would be equally convinced that they should cut down their use is doubtful.

Although the above consists of only two sentences, and in reality the attempt to persuade would be lengthier and in dialogue form, you could try to express the content of the speaker's suggestion in a more controlled and persuasive manner. You may wish to discuss suitable alterations with a partner.

EXERCISES

In order to practise your skills in persuasion of individuals and groups, use the following as causes or topics and persuade others to agree with you:

Persuading an individual

This is not a one-sided exercise as your partner should put up a resistance to your argument with arguments of his/her own. Take some time to prepare your arguments and then, without notes, start making your case. The length of time you will need is simply the time that it will take to persuade your partner of the rightness of your case!

1 Persuade a partner (who you should assume is, foolishly, a smoker) to assist you in a campaign to have the staff canteen or student common room designated as a 'No Smoking' area. This will not be a popular move but you believe strongly in the dangers of smoking and secondary inhalation.

2 Argue the case for a friend to become a vegetarian. You may wish to argue the case on health grounds or moral grounds or both.

3 Suggest to a friend who is firmly fixed on the idea of leaving school at sixteen and looking for a job that he or she should actively consider a course of further education. It would be useful for you to have as a partner somebody whose background and interests you know.

4 Try to persuade your partner, who is considering purchasing a motorbike, that it would be better to get a car licence or buy a good bicycle. You may need to research some financial and accident statistics.

5 Persuade your partner that he/she should join some organisation or cause with which you are familiar and in which you believe.

Animals' rights, vegetarianism and nuclear energy are causes that usually lead to healthy disagreement. You may need to remind yourself of some of the relevant policies and claims.

6 Argue the case with your partner that a book is generally more rewarding than a film or television programme. Make sure that you can refer to specific examples and sources.

7 Persuade your partner to take up your hobby for pleasure or profit or both. If you do not have a hobby then choose an activity that you know something about or have considered taking up yourself.

8 Persuade a partner that his/her ideas concerning sexual equality are wrong. You will need to find out the partner's views first, and then argue against them and for either the feminist or male chauvinist outlook.

When you have argued your cases then exchange roles and reverse the persuasion process. It may be better to do this some days after the original arguments.

Persuading a group

The group may be of any size from five or six to a whole room full of people. They will probably be people that you know and this can cause you even greater self-consciousness than would be the case with strangers. Take a deep breath before speaking, have all the relevant facts at your fingertips and try to appear confident.

1 Persuade the group that the radio cassette player or juke box in the common room or canteen should be played only at lunchtime and mid-session breaks. (We will assume that it is normally played without restriction.)

2 Persuade the group that all present should sign a letter you have prepared for submission to your local paper in which you take a strong stand on some contentious national or local issue of

'Excuse me, but ...'

the moment. You should use some real issue that is affecting your local community, but if you have difficulty with this you may find that the following are useful:

Whether there should be freedom of Sunday trading
That no parking restrictions be imposed in a busy area of the town
That a pedestrian precinct be established in the town centre
That a local church be turned into a bingo hall

3 Persuade the group to donate generously with time or money to a cause about which you feel strongly. You may wish the members of the group to pledge a regular amount of money or to help out with collecting in town on a Saturday morning.

4 Persuade the group to stay on after work without pay to discuss a problem that has been occurring and which you believe needs to be fully discussed for an hour or so. (Assume that it would be impossible to do this at a lunch break.)

5 Persuade the group that, if the relevant staff are willing, extra class hours be worked in order to improve performance in a subject that is causing general difficulty.

6 Persuade the group that in the interests of health and efficiency the workforce (or student body) should all follow the Japanese practice and start the working day by doing warm-up physical exercises together and then sing the national anthem or some suitably stirring song.

7 Persuade the group that the company (or school/college) should take a stand on the issue of sexual harassment. Anyone about whom there is a complaint should be suspended from work and only reinstated after a favourable finding as a result of an investigation by the management and the workers (or the principal and student representatives).

The presentation to the group should be followed by an open discussion during which questions and challenges may be made to the original speaker. You will need to have done a fair amount of background preparation to cope with spontaneous comments from the group.

5 SUMMARISING FROM NEWSPAPERS, TV AND RADIO

You may, at first, wonder what a summary of sections of the mass media has to do with spoken English communication. There are both general and particular reasons why you would benefit from developing this skill.

Personal advantages

- The act of summarising involves selecting that which is directly relevant and that which is merely illustrative. The editing decisions you need to make will be of use in developing your general skills of choice and selection.
- Reading and listening to material of topical interest in order to arrive at a summary will generally widen your interests and awareness. This is bound to be of benefit in employment as well as in life.
- Expressing another person's words in your own version of that person's message will broaden your vocabulary and make you aware of synonyms and other grammatical features. Your own use of language should become more fluent and flexible.
- When making notes for preparation of a summary of a radio or television programme your ability to make rough notes under pressure will benefit. The ability to listen and write at the same time makes you generally more mentally agile and capable of working better under pressure.
- The skills developed in organising and reorganising material to make a successful summary are of obvious benefit to your sense of structure and your decision-making powers. The awareness that a number of drafts are necessary to arrive at an acceptable end product is also to your benefit.
- The 'translation' of your summary into a fluent and persuasive piece of spoken English to a group or another individual will give you good practice in presenting a case in summary form.

Work advantages

- In a real life situation you may wish to bring to someone's attention an item that you have read, or heard on television or radio. To be able to present the essential ideas of the original in a concise and understandable form will be to your advantage both in terms of time and the impression that you make on the listener.
- In an interview for a post or for promotion it is possible that you may be asked to discuss some item of interest that you have read

recently in a newspaper. It may be that you are asked to comment on some current issue that has been discussed on radio or TV. The habit of summarising such material on paper or mentally and then relating the account to others will be of great use to you in these circumstances.

- You may be asked in an interview to summarise a process or even your career so far. The skills developed in the summary exercises that conclude this section will be directly relevant to the ability which you show, although the subject matter may be more personal.

- When an issue arises for discussion at work or in interview you will be in a strong position to deliver your ideas effectively and concisely if you have developed the habit of 'editing' material which you read and listen to.

Monastic life leaves oilmen dreaming of home comforts

Gareth Parry

FIFTEEN thousand men inhabit the 200 platforms and rigs which constitute the technologically marvellous but socially bizarre industrial province of factories, hotels and heliports which are the North Sea oilfields.

On shore, another 15,000 recuperate, counting the days to their next two-week spell of 12 hours work, 12 hours sleep, amidst the din, stench and milk chocolate-coloured mud on the drilling floor, and the eerie shrieks of gas flares.

It is all about money, from the oil companies' billions to the minimum £15,000 a year the semi-skilled "roughnecks" get for humping rusty chains and drill bits about the deck with a potential membership of what they call the "four finger club."

But while North Sea platforms are seen as potentially dangerous places — the risks have been likened to those experienced by astronauts — safety measures and awareness are considered the keenest in the West.

The heirarchy on a platform is clearly drawn. The off-shore installation manager (OIM) is in charge of everything. Next to him is the fire and safety officer who ensures that the hazardous and hostile environment is as controlled as possible. To this end drink, drugs and women are never seen on a platform (only French rigs allow wine on board).

The risk of fire is such a major pre-occupation that anyone having to use a tool, such as a hammer which could cause the slightest spark, must be authorised to do so at a specific time and location through a "hot work permit" from the fire and safety officer.

There are also mechanical, electrical and chemical experts who monitor dials and screens, and patrol the installation, check and recheck an array of production lines. Each platform also has a fully-equipped sick bay run by a para-medic.

Food, and the excellence of its cooking, which is perceived as a major component of the monastic life, is in the hands of catering staff who also maintain the spotless living quarters — the only places where smoking is allowed. Phone calls home are always available.

Platforms usually have games rooms and a gymnasium, but most men just have enough strength after a shift to drop into their bunks and think of the next helicopter home.

Fig 2   Newspaper article for summary, reproduced by kind permission of Guardian Newspapers Ltd.

Techniques of summary

a Summarising an article in a newspaper

Many journalists still follow the advice given in their training when writing a news item or feature. Such advice suggests that the writer should ensure the finished product answers the questions:

WHO? WHAT? WHEN? WHERE? and WHY?

Whether or not the writer has ensured that the article does contain the answers to these questions, as the summariser you should make efforts to discover such answers. They will probably form the basis of your summary.

Stages of summary:

1   Underline what you believe to be the key/topic/important sentences or phrases in each paragraph of the newspaper article shown in Fig 2. It is sometimes worth checking whether the opening sentence of each paragraph is a significant ' signpost' to what follows in the body of the paragraph itself.

2   When you have completed this underlining process, write down the underlined sentences and phrases exactly as they appear in the original.

3   Compare your extract of the writer's words with the whole of the original passage. Check whether the gist of the article is contained within the sentences you have written down.

4   Adjust the extracted version by the addition or subtraction of words or sentences to get the most accurate version possible.

5   Write out the version you ended up with in 4 above but *in your own words* and with any suitable additions (such as a brief introduction), eg:

'An article on the back page of yesterday's *Guardian* newspaper suggested that ...'

6   Check your version against the original article in the newspaper. Have you captured the essence of the writer's message? Have you retained relevant details?

7   If you are unhappy with your answers to the questions in 6 above then make suitable additions or subtractions.

8   Practise presenting what you have written orally and with as little use of notes as possible. It is not a good idea to learn the piece like a parrot but use your version as notes to consult when necessary.

The article that was presented at the beginning of this section might have ended up as shown in Fig 3.

Summary

The North Sea oilfield is made up of 15000 men and 200 platforms and rigs. Another 15000 men are on leave ashore on a 'fortnight on-fortnight off' system. Those on duty work a twelve-hour shift in noisy and unpleasant surroundings. The environment is highly dangerous but the minimum salary for a worker is £15000. Safety remains a high priority issue and the person in overall charge is superior only to the Fire and Safety Officer. Alcohol is banned and smoking is only allowed in the crew's living quarters. Fire is always a major concern and even to carry a tool which could accidentally cause a spark requires a special permit. Apart from the platform workers there are experts who check various technical areas of the rig as well as medical and catering staff. Leisure facilities are available but most workers are too tired to use them.
(148 words)

Fig 3

b   Summarising a television programme
It may be useful to take as our example of a suitable programme for summary a television documentary or current affairs programme. It is

such programmes that are often likely to contain material which is worth summarising for discussion with an individual or a group at work or during leisure time. The following process may be effective for you to use.

Stages of summary:

1   With a notepad and pencil, and without distractions if possible, take particular note of introductory statements of the problem or issue that is being investigated.

2   Continue to take notes, trying to recognise where there is a particular structure being used in the programme. The structure may be a 'for and against' argument or a 'chronological' arrangement of facts.

3   Make a record of any significant statistics that may be mentioned or shown. Some or all of these may be needed in your summary.

4   Take note of the names (and possibly jobs) of particular people interviewed or quoted. They may be significant contributors to the argument. At the end of the notetaking and the programme you will be able to sift out those of lesser importance.

5   Take special note towards the end of the programme of what seem to be the conclusions arrived at. There is very often a summing up at the end of a documentary programme.

6   Your summary may conclude with a brief comment of your own on the fairness of the programme's presentation and possibly what *you* believe might be a fairer conclusion based on your own experience.

c   Summarising a radio programme
It would be foolish to repeat the above guidelines, since making notes of a radio programme is not an essentially different process from that you need to adopt when dealing with TV. The same approach should be made but greater care will have to be taken with the listening process. Minute for minute there are probably more words in a radio

programme as there are no pictures to help 'tell the story'.

The use of an audio or video tape recording of a radio or television programme is beneficial if it is possible to arrange this. When you are relatively inexperienced in making notes for a later oral report it is an obvious advantage to be able to run the programme through once more in order to check the fairness and accuracy of the summary you originally made. This will allow a final, corrected or adjusted draft of your report to be made.

It is also an interesting and useful exercise to watch a recording of a programme with a group and then individually to make a summary which can be presented in turn to the rest of the group or form the basis of a group debate. Further suggestions as to the use of recordings may be found in the following exercises.

EXERCISES

1   During a period of a few days or a week make a practice of looking for interesting articles in local or national newspapers. Cut these out and, when you have a fair range of material, select one of your pieces that raises or comments on an issue on which people are likely to have differing views. Following the suggestions for summarising given earlier, make a summary and present it orally to the group.

2   Using two national newspapers, select an article or feature from each that refers to the same news event or issue. Do the summary process for each and then note the *differences* in *emphasis* and *conclusion* of each article. Combine the summaries and add your observations on these differences. You may finish by suggesting which newspaper article you feel is more accurate and why you believe this to be so. Present your 'joint summary and criticism' to the class or group.

3   Select a television or radio programme and make a summary on the lines previously suggested. Present your summary with

some final comments of your own on what you believe the programme *really* revealed and/or your own alternative view.

4   The class or group as a whole should watch a video or listen to an audio tape recording. Summaries should be made (and possibly checked by a re-run of the tape). A debate in which the summaries are used as the basis of evidence and/or supportive speeches for different viewpoints may follow up the session.

6   EXPRESSING SPECULATIVE OPINIONS

There will be times at interview and work when you will be asked to give your opinions on an issue about which you have little or no personal experience. You will be asked to speculate (or theorise) about a matter which up to that point you have not experienced in practice, eg:

As a young person who has lived at home up to the point of being interviewed you may be asked a speculative question such as:
'How do you think you would cope with living and working away from home?'

Since you can have no direct knowledge of this, it is fairly clear that the interviewer is wanting to hear both your opinion and how well you express it. The manner of answering may well be as important as the content of your answer. Such questions are asking you, without notice, to forecast or estimate an outcome. This puts you on the spot and forces you to think quickly.

Techniques for forming a suitable answer

1   Make sure that you have understood the query or question. Do not feel embarrassed at asking for clarification if necessary, eg:

'To what extent do you feel your hobbies and interests are relevant to the post in question?'

'Do you mean whether they are directly related to the specific skills required in the post, or in general terms?'

'In general and in personal terms.'

'I see. Well ...'

The candidate has checked (or clarified) the interviewer's requirements and has also had the question made slightly easier to answer. If you ask for clarification you will not be thought 'slow' – just the opposite. You will appear careful and precise. It almost goes without saying that you should not ask for clarification more often than is needed or else you may start to irritate your interviewer.

2 Recall past, relevant experience that you may be able to draw upon in arriving at your speculative answer. You may have some past experience that could form the starting point for your answer. Check quickly back in your mind and try to recall whether it worked out or whether on reflection a different course of action might have been better, eg:

'What do you think may be the biggest problem in working in one of our overseas branches?'

You think back to any other experience you have of temporarily living abroad. You recall that there were problems with the food and that you found Spanish a problem as a language. Before answering you would also be wise to clarify whether the overseas branch is in an English-speaking country.

3 Since a speculative question cannot be answered with any certainty, before replying you should consider what your questioner might believe to be an appropriate answer. It is not suggested that you tell a lie in answering but that where you see two or three possible answers you select the one that is most likely, in your opinion, to match the interviewer's, eg:

'If you had a free choice, where do you think that ideally you would like to spend your holidays?'

If you have difficulty in deciding between Greece, France and Italy, and happen to know that the company sells time share apartments in France, there is no harm in answering that France would be your first choice.

4 Once you have gone through the process of giving your speculative response do not relax too much. You should be ready for a supplementary question or challenge from the questioner. Too often the candidate or speaker is taken off guard by a follow-up question when indulging in a moment of self-congratulation at having answered satisfactorily, eg:

'What do you think is the worst aspect of having to deal with a dissatisfied customer?'
'I think that it might be having to keep your temper if they become abusive.'
'Really? You don't think that it is the sense that a potential long-term source of business to the company might be lost?'
'Well ... er ... I suppose ...'

The 'supplementary' has thrown the candidate off balance. Panic may set in.

5 Try to finish your response with a remark that suggests you are not 100 per cent sure of the answer since you have no direct experience. You should not give the impression of total insecurity but impress the questioner with the honesty of your opinion. In other words, you reserve the right (like any sensible person) to change your mind in the light of experience, eg:

'That's what I think at the moment but it is only an educated guess. I suppose my ideas might change as I gain experience.'

EXERCISE

The following role play exercises involve two people. Take it in turn to be:

- a member of staff interviewing an applicant for a college course,
  or
- an interviewer and applicant for a post in business,
  or
- two employees at a place of work.

1   A member of staff asks a student applicant what the student expects to gain from applying for a particular course, eg RSA, BTEC, GCSE.

The student answers but the interviewer comes back with a supplementary question along the lines of:

'But what makes you think that you will actually enjoy the course?'

2   An interviewer for a job asks what a candidate hopes to be doing in five years' time, assuming that the application is success-ful. The candidate should answer as best he/she can. The interviewer, dependent upon the candidate's answer, should ask a supplementary question that presents an alternative to the answer given, eg:

either 'Yes, but don't you think you might have moved on to a different company by then?'
or 'Don't you feel that you would stay with this company longer than five years?'

3   An employee asks how a fellow employee thinks he/she would take to a course in information technology, trainee management or typing.

4   A teacher asks an applicant for a course what the applicant would do with the qualifications he/she would gain in two years' time.

5   An interviewer asks a candidate for a post how the candidate will feel about constantly dealing with the public in the post applied for.

6   An employee asks another employee what could be the effect of lowering the retirement age within the company.

These are examples of the speculative type of question that you could consider with a partner. The element of surprise is obviously taken away by reading the suggested questions here. The best type of exercise and the most genuine kind of practice will be for you to take turns playing question and answer in a situation where the question is unknown until asked. You would be advised to formulate your questions within the framework of the questions already suggested as these are the areas where you are most likely to have to deal with speculative responses in your academic and working life.

SECTION 5

Assertiveness techniques

Anyone who has to deal with people is likely to benefit from developing techniques of assertiveness. Since all of us, except for the odd hermit living in the Outer Hebrides, have to deal with people at some time or another it is clear that we could all benefit. Contact with our fellow human beings takes place at home, in school, in places of leisure and at work. We shall concentrate in this section on the techniques that can be developed for effective dealings with colleagues, employers and customers in the workplace.

Once you have recognised the effectiveness of assertiveness, no doubt you will adopt similar methods in your life outside work. Even the Outer Hebridean hermit may want to assert his right to privacy from marauding television documentary crews!

The wish to adopt an assertive approach in the workplace arises when your needs and beliefs are in conflict with another's. Assertiveness allows you to reach a resolution to the conflict which leaves you feeling satisfied and the other party unresentful.

Relevant situations that arise in work might include:

- Resisting what you feel to be an unreasonable demand on your time by a superior
- Putting an unpopular request to an individual or group
- Disagreeing with a decision made by a superior
- Dealing with an awkward customer in a manner that is in the best interests of the company and yourself
- Dealing with what you believe to be inefficiency on the part of another section or department within the organisation.

Since we are not all assertive but probably have to face such situations regularly, how do we cope at present? Unfortunately we probably become very angry and allow our emotions to get a hold on us *or* we give in, appear apologetic and inwardly fume with resentment. In other words we are either *aggressive* or *non-assertive*. Neither of these is acceptable nor are they efficient alternatives to genuine assertiveness.

What is assertiveness?

It is an attitude of mind and a method of behaviour.

- It assumes recognition of the fact that you have rights (as do other people) and that you should defend your rights (as long as this is not at the expense of other people's rights)
- It is a belief in yourself and the confidence to express your opinions and feelings in an effective and appropriate manner
- It is based on the need to arrive at a conclusion satisfactory to both sides in a potential dispute

What is non-assertiveness?

It is an attitude of mind (based on lack of confidence). It is revealed by behaviour such as the following:

- Neglecting to defend personal rights and beliefs
- Adopting an apologetic and diffident manner
- Assuming the other party's rights are more significant than one's own

It is based on the assumption that dispute is best avoided by giving in.

What is aggression?

It is an attitude of mind (based on arrogance). It is revealed by behaviour such as the following:

- Considering your rights and beliefs are more important than other people's
- Adopting a belligerent manner in order to intimidate others
- Failure to recognise the possible value of other people's points of view

It is based on the assumption that getting your own way is all-important.

Situation

Let us consider how the three different attitudes would reveal themselves in a common situation.

Request: A colleague in the office, who is a personal friend, has got into the habit of asking you to make a coffee for her as your desk is nearest to the kettle and ingredients. She asks you to make her a coffee at a time when you are particularly busy.

Non-assertive response

'Well … I'm rather … you see – oh, OK. You don't take sugar do you?'

(The result is that she gets her coffee, the pattern is not broken and you quietly fume and get further behind in your work.)

Aggressive response

'You've got to be joking! Can't you see I'm busy? What did your last slave die of? Make it yourself.'

(The result is ill feeling on both sides and a friendship is in jeopardy.)

Assertive response

'I'm really very busy. I just happen to sit near the kettle. Perhaps you would like to make it for yourself.'

(The result is that your rights are defended and the unacceptable pattern is broken, with the other party getting the message about not taking advantage again.)

ADVANTAGES OF ASSERTIVENESS

1   Your point of view is recognised. It is important for your short and

long-term peace of mind as well as pride that others recognise that you have a point of view which is valuable and worthy of respect. People are much more likely to listen to you if you strike the happy medium of assertiveness rather than being a non-assertive worm or an aggressive bully.

2 Personal stress is avoided. Stress is an occupational hazard for those who fail to get to grips with assertiveness techniques. The frustration of constantly being treated like a doormat and having extra work piled on you can soon lead to distress and eventually some sort of breakdown. The alternative of confrontational aggression is not good for anybody's blood pressure!

3 Self respect is increased. Once you start to stand up for your rights instead of allowing others to take advantage you will start to feel better about yourself and the job. This increased self respect soon leads to greater self-confidence and the job becomes even more attractive.

4 Work efficiency and effectiveness is increased. A person who is constantly accepting extra burdens of work and impositions on their time is not going to work effectively. The extra work together with their hidden resentment will lead to sloppiness and hastily completed tasks. Learning how to say 'No' is often in the interests of the company as well as yourself.

5 Future conflicts are less likely to occur. Once your use of assertiveness techniques begins to be recognised by colleagues they will cease to attempt to put you in situations that are to your disadvantage. You will have broken the pattern and become known for your frankness and honesty.

RECOGNITION IN YOURSELF AND OTHERS

Individuals vary in their use of the three 'options' of verbal behaviour. It is *not* a case of a person being assertive *or* non-assertive *or* aggressive.

Until we have trained or disciplined ourselves to be generally assertive we will vary in our choice of attitude (often unaware or unconscious of how we are responding). It would be an advantage to be able to recognise which type of verbal behaviour is being used. Let us take a situation and see how a person might respond.

Situation

Request: You are working busily on a piece of work that is demanding all your attention and time. A colleague interrupts you to enquire whether you will meet him later in the day to discuss another important project that you will both be working on during the following week. You wish to postpone the discussion until the following day.

Aggressive response
'For heaven's sake, you can see that I'm busy. I'm weighed down with the work I've got on at the moment without thinking about next week's load. Get back to me later.'

Non-assertive response
'I'm so sorry ... it's just that I've got rather a lot on. I guess I take rather a long time over things. Would it be OK with you if we got together some other time tomorrow? Although I suppose if I worked over the lunch hour we could have that talk this afternoon. Which is better for you?'

Assertive response
'We could do with discussing that project. I'm too busy at the moment however. Why don't we discuss it tomorrow?'

Having looked at these 'models' of the different verbal responses, let us see what the style of the speech may reveal.

'Sorry to interrupt, but ...'

CHARACTERISTICS OF THESE RESPONSES

Aggressive

- Frequent use of *I, me, my*
- Sentences tend to be instructions or commands
- Questions, when asked, are put sarcastically
- Something that is an opinion or questionable is put as a fact
- The receiver is left feeling chastised or inferior or angry

Non-assertive

- Less use of *I, me, my*
- Tone is apologetic
- Tendency to speak in lengthy, excuse-filled sentences

- Personal feelings or needs are pushed into background
- The receiver is left feeling that an imposition has been made on the other person

Assertive

- Some use of I, *me, my*
- Tone is firm but friendly
- Use of factual statements
- Use of questions to check other person's feelings or opinions
- Opinions are not presented as facts
- The receiver is left feeling that a bargaining between equals has taken place

EXERCISE

Consider the following situations, either by yourself or with a partner, and decide whether each of the possible responses given is assertive, non-assertive or aggressive. Where there is any doubt in your mind, consider the characteristics of each and compare them with the different categories just given.

Situation A

You have arranged a meeting with a colleague to discuss some non-business matter. You are sitting in the canteen waiting for your friend. He comes in half an hour late and sits down without any apology for keeping you waiting.

'How's it going?' he asks.

You reply:

1 'Great, thanks.' (with a cheerful smile)

2 'Not so bad.' (with a slight frown)

3 'Well, I had been really looking forward to our meeting but, since I've been sitting here for half an hour, I feel rather annoyed.

After all we will not have very long to discuss our ideas now.'

4 'How's it going? How do you think it's going when you leave me sitting here like a dummy? This is really not good enough. Do you think of anyone but yourself?'

Situation B
You and Alice are colleagues in an office. She asks you to walk with her to the bus station every evening from now on as she has had an unpleasant experience recently with some street gang. You appreciate the problem but really do not want to tie yourself down to a regular commitment. You reply:

1 'That would be a great idea but I often have to drop into the library on the way home and that's in the opposite direction. I also stay on late on two or three occasions.'

2 'Well ... you see ... I suppose I could ... but ... well ... oh, OK.'

3 'What do you think I am – an escort service? You really are pushy! Forget it!'

4 'I can understand your nervousness after that experience the other evening. It was probably an isolated one, though. I'd really rather not get tied down by such an arrangement.'

5 'It must be pretty unpleasant after the incident. I couldn't make a regular commitment but I do walk that way on Friday. I could walk that way with you once a week so long as I've nothing else arranged.'

Situation C
As you are about to take your lunch break a friend calls you on the 'phone. She starts to tell you about the problems she is having with her boyfriend. You are hungry and do not want to prolong the discussion. You reply:

1 'I'd like to hear more about this later. I was just leaving the office when you rang. How would it be if I gave you a call tonight?'

2 'I'm far too busy to talk. I seem to have heard all this before. Goodbye.'

3 'Yes ... really? ... I see ... Yes ...', etc. (You listen to the whole sorry tale.)

4 'Oh not Rick again! I'm hungry, I'm tired and the whole problem leaves me cold. I'm not an agony aunt. See you.'

5 'This sounds like it will take some time to sort out. I'm just going for my lunch. You could give me a call this evening.'

Situation D
You are at a staff meeting. A man speaks to urge the meeting not to commit itself to spending money on a creche for employees' toddlers. He gives inaccurate facts in order to persuade the meeting to his point of view. You do not agree with his views. Your reaction is:

1 You get to your feet and say, 'You're lying. You haven't a clue what you're talking about.'

2 You say nothing.

3 You quietly tell the person next to you how angry you feel at listening to the speaker.

4 You get to your feet and say, 'Well, I don't know too much about this as I'm not a mother. I feel that although the facts just given seem to indicate ... , well ...'

5 You get to your feet and say, 'We've heard one viewpoint and I must say that I disagree with it. I would like to give my points in support of a creche ...'

DEVELOPING YOUR SKILLS IN ASSERTIVENESS

The best way to develop the necessary attitude and confidence is actually to practise being assertive. Every day provides us with situations, both major and minor, when we have a choice of how to behave and react.

There are three general guidelines to remember when developing the correct frame of mind for assertive speech and behaviour:

1 Adopt a manner that allows the other person to know that you *understand* him/her and that you respect his/her *rights*.

2 Ensure that the other person knows how *you* feel about a situation.

3 Make sure that you let the other person know what *you* want.

Before setting a number of role play exercises for you to practise by yourself or with a partner, it is worth examining another aspect of assertiveness which involves non-verbal communication.

Just as there are verbal mannerisms that allow you to identify whether you or an opposite number are behaving assertively, non-assertively or aggressively, the body can send similar signals by tone, expression, eye movement and body movement. The following simple pointers are worth watching for:

Non-verbal signals (body language)

Tone (of voice)
- Aggressive: hard, sarcastic, raised, chilly, unfriendly
- Non-assertive: either over-gentle or dull and monotonous, slightly tremulous, rather quiet and timid
- Assertive: clear, honest, warm, neither raised nor quiet, steady

Expression (of face)
- Aggressive: frowns, occasional sarcastic smile, teeth clenched or chin jutting, eyebrows raised in query

- Non-assertive: nervous or hesitant smile at inappropriate time, generally nervous or worried expression, rapidly changing mouth movements
- Assertive: open, honest smile or frown when mood changes, chin relaxed, face composed

Eyes (movement and contact)
- Aggressive: dominating, tending to try to outstare you, fixed look
- Non-assertive: shifty, downcast, rapid eye movement (blinking)
- Assertive: firm, eye contact made but not a 'staring match'

Body (movement)
- Aggressive: generally rigidly upright or leaning forward towards receiver, tends to point finger or thump furniture for emphasis, head held high, often moves around while speaking, hands held on hips or arms crossed firmly
- Non-assertive: generally stooped, hunched and defensive, tends to withdraw from close proximity, may cover mouth with hand tendency to general nervous movements and is often in some sort of unsteady or shuffling stance or posture
- Assertive: relaxed upright stance held up but not high, measured movements and generally open receptive appearance

It goes almost without saying that you are unlikely to witness *all* of these non-verbal signals at one and the same time between just two people! Get into the habit of observing people's non-verbal signals and you will soon start to recognise or be conscious of them in your own behaviour. Obviously you will want only to adopt consciously the mannerisms that signal 'assertive person'.

ROLE PLAY EXERCISES

Using a partner to check and criticise the assertiveness of your response, try to react appropriately in the following situations. Discuss with your partner the degree of assertiveness that was achieved in your response to the situation. In each case change roles so that you both have experience of listening and judging as well as being on the receiving end of assertive behaviour. It is possible to use these situations as solo role plays but in that case the use of a tape recorder is recommended so that you can check back on your performance.

Situations

1   A colleague has volunteered your services as secretary of a staff leisure association in your absence. You are not too keen on either the unofficial post or being volunteered without consultation. You meet the colleague and say ...

2   A customer comes into the retail shop where you are on duty and complains of a faulty appliance that was purchased from the shop. Its guarantee has run out by five days. The customer is in a very bad mood. You say ...

3   You are in charge of a reprographics department in a business organisation. You realise that the photocopier is being used for personal copying at the firm's expense. You do not know who is 'guilty'. You have to try to control the situation. At a staff meeting you stand up and say ...

4   A colleague had arranged to attend a meeting with you. He failed to turn up and you were left in a difficult situation. You meet the colleague the next day. You say ...

5   A junior member of staff has asked you to give her more responsibility. She is not coping very well with the responsibilities she already has. You say ...

6   You are having difficulty with a piece of work that you have to complete shortly. There is someone in the department that has previous experience of the type of work with which you are having difficulty. You need this person's help. You approach the person and say ...

7 You are on the 'phone to a rather important client. You are interrupted in mid call by a junior member of staff seeking your advice on a relatively unimportant matter. You cover the mouthpiece of the phone and say ...

8 Your employer comes in just before you are due to go home at the end of the day. He asks you to do some urgent last-minute work. You have arranged to meet someone who is waiting for you in town. The meeting is important to you. You turn to your employer and say ...

9 A colleague asks to borrow your dictionary. This colleague is notorious for being something of an absent-minded scrounger. You say ...

10 A sales representative is pushing you rather hard to place an order. You do not want to commit yourself until you have checked a rival product. The sales representative starts to push very hard. You say ...

11 You have just started to do some work on the photocopier. A manager from another department asks you if you would mind running off a few copies of a document for him as he is rather busy. Your manager is also waiting and in something of a hurry. You say ...

12 Your employer has asked a member of staff who is junior to you, and also inexperienced, to be responsible for a piece of work. You are already aware that the piece of work is being done wrongly and you also feel that you have been bypassed. You see your employer and say ...

13 A new member of staff has started to arrive for work unpunctually. He always seems to have some plausible excuse. You see him in a crowded canteen and say ...

14 You are queuing at the counter of the staff canteen. It is your turn to be served but another colleague from another department puts himself forward. You turn to him and say ...

15 Your office is particularly busy as a staff audit is due. A subordinate asks permission to be absent from work the next day to visit a relative who is sick in hospital. This will place an added burden on the rest of the staff. You happen to know that the relative is very dear to this person who is requesting time off. The situation is tricky but the decision is yours ...

16 A member of staff senior to yourself has rather unpleasant racist views that are publicly aired at every opportunity. Although nobody else seems to share your annoyance you are getting increasingly angry. A remark that you find offensive is made on one of his visits to the general office. You say ...

17 Although there are no anti-smoking regulations in operation in your office, a colleague tends to smoke excessively when the pressure of work builds up. You object to this because of the dangers of secondary inhalation as well as the smell. You know of at least one other member of the office staff who feels the same way as you. Another cigarette has just been lit. You say ...

18 Your manager is in the habit of making rather crude jokes when in your presence. These are always rather suggestive and you do not welcome what have clearly become personal advances. Things come to a head when he makes a crude remark in the lift at the end of the day. The lift is crowded. You turn to him and say ...

19 A new position has been created in the company for which you work. It would mean a promotion for you. Your qualifications are just about relevant to the new position. It has been indicated that anyone in the firm who is interested should have a preliminary meeting with the personnel director. You meet him in the corridor and say ...

20   At a full staff meeting a senior member of staff has just made a joke which is sexist and stereotypes women. You find the joke tasteless. The person concerned is notorious for his chauvinistic views. He is the managing director's son-in-law. You stand up and say ...

There are many more situations that you, a partner or the group can devise. A discussion in which individuals offer personal experiences where assertiveness would have been valuable will raise a lot of role plays that you can rehearse. You should remember that there is no such being as the totally and consistently assertive person. From time to time and from situation to situation we all range from non-assertive through to aggressive.

With practice you will come to realise that assertiveness gains you better results and raises your self-esteem as well as your self-confidence. The ultimate result of this is that you become a more efficient employee and a more effective human being.

Oral skills and the telephone

The telephone can be either a great asset to a company or a handicap. It is the user's standard of effectiveness that creates the distinction. A telephone is dangerous in that, in bad hands, it seems to amplify all the faults and dangers that are lurking in oral communication.

The removal of the visual element prevents us from sending or receiving all the subtle, visual signals that are a part of the communication process. The mechanical/electronic reproduction of the voice removes the subtle shifts in tone and pitch that can make all the difference to interpretation of the spoken word. We must take great care when using the telephone, especially in a business context.

SOME BASIC GUIDELINES FOR TELEPHONE USE

When answering a call

1 When answering the telephone you should adopt a friendly and welcoming tone.

2 The caller should be given the number and name of the organisation or department so that the caller quickly realises if a wrong number has been dialled.

3 Conversations should last only for as long as necessary.

4 Notes should be taken (preferably on a message pad) for further action that might be required.

5   Always make sure that you take down or ask for details of the caller's name, job, business, telephone number and extension number unless they are well known to your company and on record.

6   Check, by repetition if necessary, any details that you are taking down. You may feel that this is slowing down the call but it is only efficient and better than passing on an incomplete or inaccurate message.

7   Before you pass on the call – if this is what the caller wants – politely check what the caller's business is so that you can be sure you are giving the call to the right person.

8   If you are taking a message or taking down details, repeat the main points of the message to the caller at the end of the call to give an opportunity for verification and checking.

9   When the call is over make a legible copy of the notes taken. These are either for yourself or for the person to whom you may have to forward the message.

10   Make sure that you pass on the message if this applies. During the course of a day it would be very easy to forget a phone call made hours earlier.

When making a call

You should ensure that these guidelines are followed:

1   Decide what you are calling about. Do not be vague about the purpose of your call. If necessary, make a note of the points you wish to communicate.

2   Make sure you have a notepad to hand to take down any details.

3   Try to discover the precise name or title of the person to whom you need to speak before you make the call. This will make it much

easier for the switchboard operator or receiver of the call to put you in
contact quickly.

4 Don't dial a wrong number. Check the number beforehand and
dial it or ask for it carefully.

5 When the call gets through give your name and business clearly so
that the other party can know whom to contact if the call should be cut
off or a reply required later.

6 Offer spellings of any important details. These could be names,
addresses and any special brand or product names.

7 Repeat any numbers that are given by you in the conversation.

8 Ensure that the receiver of your call has understood the details
given or requested. You may ask them to repeat important details of
your message or request to you.

9 Politely thank the receiver of your call for his/her help and time.

10 Act on any information that the call has revealed. Do not
mentally file what the call has revealed as it could be difficult to
remember at the end of a busy day.

How *not* to use the telephone

The call taker is finishing making a check on something that has just
been written. The phone rings.

  'Can you hold on a second?'
  The call taker cradles the phone against a shoulder and finishes
checking the typing, keeping the call maker waiting, and then says:
  'Can I help you?'
  'The boss isn't in at the moment.'
  'I can find out. Hang on.'

'Not yours? Mavis must have got the address wrong again!'

'About three o'clock.'
'I'll try and tell him if I see him.'
'You'll ring back?'
'OK. See you.'

Check the above one side of the dialogue against the guidelines given for receiving a call. Which of these have been broken or ignored? Have you *really* never had someone speak to you on the telephone in this way? Have *you* ever acted like this when receiving a call?

TELEPHONE ROLE PLAY EXERCISES

The only really effective way to become skilled in using the telephone is to practise with a number of partners in situations that might genuinely arise.

All that is required is a room where two desks or tables can be placed at some distance apart and two handsets be put on these. The telephone handsets can be either working or 'dummies'. It is ideal if the handsets can be connected so that the genuine sound of a telephone is achieved but this is by no means essential.

The call maker and the call taker are seated back to back at the handsets and provided with notepad and pencil. It is important that the role players cannot look at each other. The denial of the opportunity for visual signals is important in recreating the authenticity and difficulty of a real telephone call.

A third party or a group should witness the calls as they take place so that criticism may be made at the end of the role play to help the call maker and call taker. The group can also learn a lot by observing the strengths and weaknesses of others.

Although the situations all refer to 'you', it takes two people to have a telephone conversation (unless you *like* talking to answering machines!). In every case your partner should play the role of the opposite party. If you play each party in each situation you will develop skills as both call maker and call taker, as well as being able to compare different ways of handling a call, based on each other's performance.

Situation

1 Call a friend to let him/her know of an accident that has happened to a classmate. The call taker should ask for details of how the accident happened. The call maker should suggest a visit to the friend in hospital. An arrangement is made to meet in town at a particular time and place. Ensure that the last arrangements are clearly understood by both parties.

2 Ring a friend to ask if he/she has a video tape recorder. Having discovered that the friend does have a VTR, request that a recording is made of a particular programme. Give all the required details (programme, channel, day, time, etc) that will allow the recording to be made. Finish by making arrangements to collect the completed tape.

3 You need to discuss arrangements with a classmate for an end of term surprise party for your class teacher. You telephone to see if your friend will meet you before classes commence the next day. Arrange a precise time and place as well as agreeing a possible venue for the party.

4 You ring a local 'unit' cinema to find out what is playing. You are given the titles of four films. You make a booking and enquire the precise times of showing and you receive details of when tickets should be picked up.

5 You have lost your copy of this book. You need to order a new copy from a local bookshop. Telephone the bookshop and supply the necessary information for a successful order to be placed (title, author, publisher, ISBN number, your address). Your partner should ensure that all the required information has been successfully received, checked and noted.

6 At a party held at a friend's house you were very impressed by a particular dish which was part of a buffet. You ring your friend to give your thanks and to enquire as to the recipe for the dish. Your friend dictates the outline of the recipe and the ingredients.

7 It is late at night and the telephone rings. It is a person in your class who has become something of a nuisance, constantly seeking your advice about trouble that is being experienced with a friend. You do not want to encourage these telephone calls or the general pestering that has developed. Your caller is apparently upset. Deal with the call assertively.

8 Telephone a friend to ask for instructions on how to get from the town bus station to the Job Centre on foot. Your friend will give suitable instructions and you will take a note of them. Checks should be made whenever necessary.

9 You wish to ask a teacher if you can give his/her name as a referee on a job application form. You telephone to see if this is acceptable. The teacher enquires briefly about the nature of the job. The teacher then agrees and you enquire about his/her home address and telephone number for the application form.

10   You are going for a job interview in London. You will need bed and breakfast accommodation for the night before the interview. You telephone a hotel to check the rates and then make a booking. You should also check which is the nearest public transport to the hotel.

11   You receive a call when at work from the wife of your manager. She wants to speak to him about a minor domestic crisis with the plumbing. You know that he is in an important meeting and does not wish to be disturbed. Deal with the call as you think fit.

12   You take a call from a customer who is very upset at the failure of a product purchased at the retail shop where you work. The caller is aggressive but it is your duty to try to do your best for the shop's interests. Deal with the call in such a way that you keep your self-respect and take account of the interests of the shop as well as the needs of the customer.

13   You receive a call from an important executive who is due to visit your company the following day. She is staying at a hotel/conference centre in the town. She wishes to be given instructions on how to drive from there to your place of business (you may use your school or college as the point to which you are directing her). She would also like your manager to ring her the same evening. Check that you have the right number.

14   A caller wishes to speak to your manager, who is away at a trade fair. The caller wants to get in touch with him/her urgently. Your manager has said that he/she only wants to be contacted in an emergency. Deal with the call as assertively as you believe to be appropriate.

15 You receive a call from an employee's doctor. An appointment has previously been made that needs to be changed. You take down the required details for passing on to the employee concerned.

16 You receive a call from a subordinate in your department at work. He says that he cannot get in to work this morning as he has made an appointment for later in the day to have an injection. The injection is required so he may travel abroad for his summer holidays later in the year. There is a meeting that you would have liked him to attend the same morning. Deal with the call assertively.

17 Decorators have been repainting the administrative area of the company where you work. Your manager had discovered that his office has been painted 'mushroom' when he specified in writing that he wanted 'magnolia'. He asks you to 'phone the decorators and demand a free repaint. The call taker tries to deny responsibility on the part of the decorators.

18 You receive a call from a business person who was a visitor to your company a few days before. The caller thinks that his address book has been accidentally left on the premises. He asks you to check and you do this. The book is not in the lost property drawer. You take his details in case it turns up later.

19 A colleague in the office has started a nose bleed which apparently refuses to stop. You know that a member of staff who works in another annexe is trained in First Aid. You call this person and explain the situation. The symptoms are demanded and, after giving these, you request simple First Aid advice. Appropriate information is given to you.

20 A colleague has taken three days' leave of absence. You need to request him/her to return to work a day early because of a problem that has arisen at work. The colleague does not wish to

give up the last day (which is his/her right). Both call maker and
call taker should behave assertively and/or persuasively.

21   An incomplete order of office stationery has been received by
your company from the suppliers. You need the missing items to
be delivered as soon as possible. You call the supplier in order to
complain and to try to get the order delivered the following day.
The delivery truck would not normally be in your area for another
week. Negotiate.

22   A visitor to your place of work has been knocked down in the
car park by one of your delivery vans.You witness this through the
window. The victim is lying on the ground, apparently unconscious. People are at the scene of the accident. You decide to call
999. Make the call – efficiently.

23   One of your colleagues has been taken ill and needs to go
home. There is nobody available to drive her and she cannot travel
by public transport. Ring her husband at his place of work and
state the situation. Make suitable arrangements.

24   You have been asked by your manager if you will take her
place at a weekend conference. You had arranged to visit a friend
on the weekend in question but could postpone this. You would
really rather not go to the conference. You decide to call her and
negotiate assertively.

25   The company finance officer needs to know the registration
numbers of two of the company cars so that he can arrange their
insurance. He rings you with this request and, after asking him to
'hold', you supply him with the required information. The numbers
are E649 TCK and B334 BTD.

SPEAKING CLEARLY

In cases where an address or a name is being spoken or dictated over
the telephone it may be necessary to ensure that the spelling is correct.

The line may be a bad one or the other person may not be totally familiar with English. The 'telephone alphabet' can be of assistance in such cases.

Telephone alphabet – standard letter analogy

This is the alphabet most commonly used and understood by the average person

A	Alfred	J	Jack	S	Samuel
B	Benjamin	K	King	T	Tommy
C	Charlie	L	London	U	Uncle
D	David	M	Mary	V	Victor
E	Edward	N	Nellie	W	William
F	Frederick	O	Oliver	X	X-ray
G	George	P	Peter	Y	Yellow
H	Harry	Q	Queen	Z	Zebra
I	Isaac	R	Robert		

Radio telephone alphabet – formal

as used by police and air traffic control

A	Alpha	J	Juliette	S	Sierra
B	Bravo	K	Kilo	T	Tango
C	Charlie	L	Lima	U	Uniform
D	Delta	M	Mike	V	Victor
E	Echo	N	November	W	Whisky
F	Foxtrot	O	Oscar	X	X-ray
G	Golf	P	Papa	Y	Yankee
H	Hotel	Q	Quebec	Z	Zulu
I	India	R	Romeo		

Using the latter telephone alphabet the word *cat* would be dictated as 'C for Charlie, A for Alpha, T for Tango '.

Using one or other of the telephone alphabet systems, spell out aloud your own name. You only need to use the system if there is a word that is causing difficulty over the telephone or if the caller asks you to spell something out.

Finally, a few words about pronouncing numbers so that they are not misheard over the telephone. Apart from aiming to speak with clarity and at a sensible pace, the following pronunciation of numbers is accepted generally for telephone use:

Pronouncing numbers

0	oh	(long *o* sound)
1	wun	(emphasis on *n*)
2	too	(emphasis on *t* with drawn out *oo*)
3	thr-r-ee	(a rolled *r* and extended *ee*)
4	foer	(long *o* sound)
5	fife	(stress on first *f*)
6	sixe	(long *x* sound)
7	sev-en	(two distinct syllables)
8	ate	(long *a* sound and stressed *t*)
9	nine	(one syllable with long *I* and stressed first *n*)

As seen at the beginning of this section, a telephone can be a great asset, but it can also be a time waster and a means of causing confusion and ambiguity. To be more accurate, it is the users of telephones that cause confusion and ambiguity. With practice you will become one of those who use the phone as a means of extending their skills of communication and so increase your usefulness and effectiveness in the world of work.

Index